The Beginning Naturalist
Weekly Encounters with the Natural World

The Beginning Naturalist

Weekly Encounters with the Natural World

by
Gale Lawrence

Illustrated
by
Adelaide Murphy

The New England Press
Shelburne, Vermont

Second printing, August 1984
Third printing, June 1986
Fourth printing, April 1988
Fifth printing, August 1991

The New England Press
P.O. Box 525
Shelburne, Vermont 05482

Library of Congress Catalog Card Number: 79-89171
ISBN: 0-933050-02-X

PRINTED IN THE UNITED STATES OF AMERICA

An Invitation

A walk in the outdoors is, for me, always a pleasure. I relish it no matter what the weather or the season.

Occasionally I'm fortunate to have a companion along. Together we ponder the fate of that trout fighting its way upstream, or the chances for that sapling overshadowed by larger forest trees. And to look and consider all the hundreds of such events with a friend just doubles my pleasure.

Gale Lawrence is just such a friend. Through the magic of the words on these pages she takes you on one delightful stroll after another. Here you stand by a frozen pond and wonder about the beavers down beneath the ice. There you watch the heartbreak of a small bird separated from its parents.

You stand, breathless, listening to the mysterious sounds of a night in the woods. Then, on a summer day, you practically cheer as a struggling creature escapes its dull brown nymphal case and becomes that alert and shimmering aerial predator—the dragonfly.

Gale's talented pen invites you for a walk through the pungent autumn foliage on a search for butternuts. She lets you predict your own winter as you contemplate the color pattern of a woolly bear caterpillar. Then, just as you congratulate yourself as a flawless weather prophet, she hits you with an icy arctic blast.

The woolly bear, as she points out, will have none of this foolishness. It merely curls up and sleeps all winter.

It is all here—pressed down and running over—fifty-two delightful outings with an articulate, friendly companion who bears a twinkle in her eye. Gale Lawrence knows so well what I, too, have discovered: while sorrow sometimes may be borne alone, joy must be shared.

I am glad she has shared it with me in inviting me to write these few words. And now I pass along this new found joy: you come for a walk, too.

Ronald Rood
June, 1979

Introduction

Many people want to know more about nature, but they don't know where to begin. The subject simply overwhelms them. Birds are too numerous and move too fast to identify easily. Flowers come in so many shapes and colors that the prospect of learning all their names seems overwhelming. And then there are insects, ferns, and trees—not to mention amphibians, reptiles, and mammals—whose names might be familiar but whose ways of life are a complete mystery. Not only is nature awesome in its variety and complexity, but time to learn about it seems all too short. Where, then, should a beginner begin?

Several years ago I moved from Washington, D.C., back to my native Vermont. During the time I had lived in the city, nature had always seemed vaguely important to me, but other priorities of one kind or another had always kept it toward the bottom of my list. Now, back in Vermont, hardly a day passed when I was not brought face-to-face with a natural phenomenon. Almost without thinking, I found myself starting to pay closer attention to my surroundings. I began to feel an urgency to learn about nature.

About that time I decided to become a volunteer at the Green Mountain Audubon Nature Center located just down the road from my house. I soon discovered that the nature center needed not just volunteers but knowledgeable trail guides who could teach busloads of school children something meaningful about the natural world. Before I knew it, I was on the trail with a dozen inquisitive children behind me. They asked me basic, essential, and important questions about the workings of nature: Where does soil come from? What do worms eat? Why are there so many bugs? Why do some animals kill other animals? Their questions were good ones. I, too, wanted to know the answers.

My search for answers taught me that in order to learn more about nature I needed to focus my attention on one subject at a time and to ask specific questions about it. I decided, therefore, that each week throughout the year I would learn more about one particular subject that had provoked my curiosity that week. Maybe it was that annoying mosquito that bit me while I was trying to go to sleep, or a spider web that had not existed the day before, or a child's question that had left me wondering. Whatever the subject or the provocation for learning about it, I pursued the subject until my questions were answered. I read, made careful observations, took notes, and tried through writing about the subject to make meaning out of what before had been vague or chaotic.

The most important advantage to this one-subject-at-a-time approach is that eventually my knowledge began to spiral. Each new subject added new insights to old subjects, and all the old subjects provided, and continue to provide, background for the new subjects.

This book is a collection of fifty-two short essays that tell of my encounters with nature during the past two years. Almost all of them have appeared in one form or another in local newspapers. My weekly observations start with the winter solstice because that is where I began.

You may begin where I do or at any other point in the book. Like nature itself, the sequence of the book is not rigid. Where you begin is not important. What does matter is that you begin—that you begin to look at what's around you, ask yourself questions about what you see, and find answers. Only in this way will you establish a meaningful and lasting relationship with the natural world—of which you, too, are an important part.

CONTENTS

MIDWINTER TO MUDTIME

1	Winter Birds	3
2	Winter Mammals	8
3	Winter Insects	11
4	Winter Trees	15
5	Woodpeckers	18
6	Snow	22
7	Groundhogs	25
8	Porcupines	30
9	Beavers	34
10	Spiders	38
11	Maple Sap	42
12	Redpolls	44
13	Pussy Willows	47

SPRING INTO SUMMER

14	Foxes	53
15	Edible Wild Foods	56
16	The Frog Run	60
17	Robins	65
18	Wood Ducks	67
19	Woodcocks	71

20	Dandelions	74
21	Tent Caterpillars	78
22	Baby Birds	81
23	Soil	86
24	Red Efts	90
25	Mosquitoes	93
26	Dragonflies	97

SUMMER

27	Fireflies	103
28	Buttercups	107
29	Bees, Wasps, and Hornets	110
30	Ants	113
31	Raspberries	117
32	Galls	120
33	Queen Anne's Lace	123
34	Cattails	127
35	Slugs	131
36	Centipedes and Millipedes	135
37	Shrews	138
38	Ladybugs	141
39	Hawks	144

FALL AND WINTER AGAIN

40	Earthworms	153
41	Nocturnal Animals	157

42	Chipmunks	160
43	Hares	163
44	Woolly Bears	166
45	Butternuts	169
46	Club Mosses	172
47	Lichens	176
48	Birds' Nests	180
49	Goldfinches	184
50	Birches	188
51	Nuthatches	192
52	The Big Dipper	195

EPILOGUE   198

RESOURCES FOR THE
   BEGINNING NATURALIST   201

INDEX   205

Midwinter
to
Mudtime

1

Winter Birds

If you've been leading an indoor life but have been wanting to spend more time outdoors, don't wait until spring. Bundle up and take advantage of the cold winter months to start learning about nature. Winter, in fact, is an excellent time to begin. Many birds have migrated south. Many mammals are sleeping. Reptiles and amphibians are hibernating, and therefore can be ignored until spring. Insects are in a condition similar to hibernation, called diapause.

The plant kingdom is also simplified. Many plants have either died or withdrawn into their roots, where they will remain dormant for the winter. Leaves are gone from most trees, so you can examine their basic shapes and look closely at their twigs and buds. In short, nature is almost manageable for a beginner during the long, inactive weeks of December, January, and February.

If you'd like to begin learning about nature this winter, the first thing you might do is put up a bird feeder near a window. Invite winter birds close to your house in order to see them better. If you offer sunflower seeds, you will probably be visited very shortly by black-capped chickadees, blue jays, and evening grosbeaks.

Chickadees are the most numerous visitors to my bird feeder. I must have over a dozen of them who are regulars. I call them "one-at-a-timers" because each flies in, grabs a seed, and flies to a perch nearby to eat it. They remind me of a busy airport with planes landing and taking off as fast as the control tower will let them.

My second most numerous visitors are blue jays. I had always thought of blue jays as somewhat ugly—perhaps because they are noisy and aggressive. When I saw them up close I was surprised to discover what a beautiful shade of blue they are. Their stark black, white, and blue markings are actually very handsome.

Blue jays come to the feeder to eat or to stock up on seeds. If a blue jay is on a supply mission it will gobble up fourteen or fifteen seeds. When it has as many seeds as it can cram into its mouth and throat, it will fly off to hide its treasures. This hoarding accounts for the disappearance of many of my sunflower seeds.

EVENING GROSBEAK

Evening grosbeaks are large, mustard-yellow birds with

black markings. They have strong seed-cracking beaks. They travel in flocks, and when they visit a feeder they drive the chickadees, blue jays, and other birds away. An evening grosbeak is a gluttonous eater—it perches on the feeder and eats seed after seed, strewing the shells every which way in its haste.

Evening grosbeaks are an interesting species. In response to the food available in bird feeders they have altered their natural feeding and nesting habits. Winter feeding has invited them into areas where they never lived before. Some people don't like evening grosbeaks because they are domineering and seem to eat more than their fair share of seeds. I have even heard them referred to as "feeder bums."

If in addition to sunflower seeds you offer mixed seeds, you will be inviting other birds to your feeders. I offer only sunflower seeds at one window and mixed seeds at another. I also throw some mixed seeds on top of a low wooden storage box that's just outside my front door. The mixed seeds bring redpolls, juncos, tree sparrows, and pine siskins.

I also hang an onion bag of suet in a shrub that's close to my sunflower feeder. The suet is appealing to some of the seed-eaters, but it also attracts woodpeckers. Making the distinction between the downy and the hairy woodpecker can be your first exercise in close observation. The hairy woodpecker is bigger than the downy and has a longer bill. Otherwise they are almost identical.

If you are serious about learning to identify your bird visitors by name, especially the small look-alikes that come for mixed seed, you should buy yourself a field guide. Most field guides include both pictures and descriptive information to help you determine the name of the bird you're looking at. You will have to pay close attention to size, color, shape, and distinctive markings. You might find binoculars helpful when it comes to small details like eye rings, wing bars, and patches of color.

Once you've had some practice identifying the wood-peckers and seedeaters right outside your windows, you'll be ready for the new birds returning in the spring. It will take you much longer than a year to master all the warblers, sparrows, and thrushes you'll see, but once you start paying attention to birds you'll be hooked. Learning about them won't seem like work anymore.

One note of caution: if you decide to feed wild birds during the winter, consider yourself committed. The birds will come to depend on the food you offer them, and it isn't fair to stop feeding them during the lean winter months when wild food is scarce. If you had never fed them they would have spread out in search of food. The seeds in your feeder are now part of the food supply that supports the local population. If your seeds disappear, there's not enough food to go around, and that means some birds will starve.

Other birds stay in the North through the winter, but you won't see them at your feeders. You'll have to go out looking for them, and even then you may never see them. Walking in the woods you may scare up a ruffed grouse, and it will probably scare you as much as you scare it—the sudden rush of wings is always a surprise. Ruffed grouse survive the winter by eating wild seeds, nuts, and buds they find in the woods.

Owls are around too, but they're hard to see because they're nocturnal. Another difference between owls and the feeder birds is that owls are predators: they prefer mice and rabbits to seeds and suet. Listen for owls at about the time the sun goes down or after dark, and watch for one if you hear crows or bluejays making a racket around a tree.

While you're beginning to watch and listen outdoors, learn the sounds a chickadee makes. If you hear one nearby, frequently you can call it in close to where you're standing by talking to it and making pshhh-wshhh-wshhh sounds. When it comes to look you over it may bring friends and may even introduce you to a nuthatch.

Other familiar birds you may notice during the winter are the resourceful scavengers—gulls and crows—and the imported species—pigeons and house sparrows.

If you become interested enough in watching birds to want to keep track of what you're seeing, a state agency, an Audubon Society, or a local nature center may have a checklist of all the birds in your area. While the checklists don't describe the birds or tell you where to find them, they do indicate relative abundance and seasonal status. You'll find that these local checklists nicely complement your more comprehensive field guide.

Watching winter birds is only one way to acquaint yourself with the natural world. But the nice thing about birds is that they will invite you to notice many other things—such as the trees they perch in and the plant and animal food they eat. Finally, an interest in birds will help you begin to understand how everything interacts in the natural world.

2

Winter Mammals

Winter is also a good time to learn something about your fellow mammals. Like winter birds, winter mammals are fewer in kind—not because they've migrated, but because many of them have disappeared into their holes, nests, or dens to wait out the cold weather.

Some mammals hibernate—they fall into a deep sleep for the entire winter. Woodchucks, some bats, and jumping mice are hibernators, so you won't see any signs of them at all.

Some mammals are sleepers rather than hibernators. They sleep for weeks at a time, but then they wake up and scout around for a meal. Chipmunks save themselves the trouble of having to leave home. They store food right inside their snug underground burrows. They disappear so completely during the winter that many people think of them as hibernators. Raccoons, skunks, and bears sleep for long periods, but they don't store food—they wake up occasionally and prowl around for a meal.

Winter is not a hardship to either the sleepers or the hibernators. Rather, it's the animal that remains active that has the problems. It needs food to stay alive, and the tracks it leaves in the snow identify it and tell of its struggle to find enough to eat. One set of tracks may show you where a mouse has raced all over the surface of the snow picking up seeds that have fallen from trees. Another set of tracks may show you where a group of deer rested or where they pawed in the snow for acorns. You may also see the tracks of a predator chasing its prey, or the scene of a tussle with a few feathers or bits of fur to identify the deceased.

You can begin to learn animal tracking with your dog's or cat's tracks or even human footprints. Look closely at familiar tracks to see what they can tell you about the direction the animal (or person) was headed, about its size, and about its rate of speed. You can experiment with your own tracks. First walk, then jog, then run as fast as you can. If you examine the different tracks you will be able to see how they change when your pace changes.

One of the first details you may notice about familiar animal tracks is that dogs walk with their toenails out, cats with their claws in. Cats also walk very tidily in a straight line, whereas domestic dogs tend to leave sloppy tracks.

After you've mastered the tracks of neighborhood dogs and cats, you may want to take a walk in the woods to look for fox or deer tracks, or visit a brook to look for signs of mink. Other animals that are active throughout the winter include shrews, moles, meadow mice, deer mice, weasels, fishers, coyotes, squirrels, porcupines, hares, and rabbits.

It will help you find the tracks you're looking for or understand the tracks you see if you know what the different animals eat. Some mammals are looking for plant food—seeds, nuts, bark, twigs, frozen fruit, or buds—while other mammals are looking for each other. The deer mouse, for instance, spends most of its waking hours looking for seeds, nuts, and acorns—while fishers, weasels, minks, coyotes, foxes, bobcats, and owls are looking for deer mice.

One way to understand the complex relationships between the eaters and the eaten is to learn some food chains. Seed-mouse-fox is one such food chain; bark-hare-coyote is another. But eating in the wild is never that simple. The plant eaters depend on many different plant foods, and the predators prey on many different plant eaters. The overlapping and interdependent food chains create a food web.

Learning what animals eat and identifying their tracks is not simple, but it's addictive. You'll need books to help you. One useful book is *American Wildlife and Plants: A Guide to Wildlife Food Habits* (New York: Dover Publications, 1961). Another is the Peterson Series *Field Guide to Animal Tracks* (Boston: Houghton Mifflin, 1954). Both books are comprehensive, referring to animals that live in all parts of the country. Your local nature center might have a guide to just the animals in your area.

Paying attention to animal tracks in winter will teach you a great deal about the animals' behavior—what they eat, where they live, and how far they roam. When the snow melts you can continue your tracking in the mud, and you will begin to notice some new tracks. The mammals that were sleeping or hibernating will become active again. And then, as mud turns into dust, you may begin to notice some smaller tracks—the miniature tracks of the young.

3

Winter Insects

Did you ever stop to think where insects go during the winter months? Some insects, like the white-faced hornets that make the football-size nests you see hanging in trees, die when the cold weather hits. Only the fertile queens survive to start new colonies in the spring. Honeybees remain alive and active, but they stay hidden in their hives where they've stored honey for winter food. Monarch butterflies migrate, some flying all the way to Mexico for the winter.

Many insects, when the days begin to shorten in the fall, enter a state much like suspended animation called *diapause*. In diapause, activities are reduced to a bare minimum. The insect's metabolism becomes even slower than that of a mammal, reptile, or amphibian in hibernation. A diapausal insect is just barely alive.

Some familiar insects such as houseflies, mosquitoes, and ladybugs enter diapause as adults. Other insects are at different stages of their three- or four-stage life cycles when winter comes. Praying mantises, for example, lay eggs in the fall with "programmed instructions" for them not to hatch until the days lengthen in the spring. Then the adults die.

An interesting little engineer called the maple leaf cutter winters in the second stage of its life cycle, during which it is called a *larva*. The larva makes a round, pill-size sandwich from two pieces of maple leaf. It spends the winter inside its small round sandwich, which has fallen to the leaf litter on the forest floor.

Some of the large silk moths such as the lunas and cecropias spend the winter in the third stage of their life cycle. They are then called *pupae*. The pupal stage is a time of rest between the eating-and-growing larval stage and mature adulthood. It is during this stage that the insect's body changes from a wormlike caterpillar into the winged adult. Luna and cecropia moths spend the winter snug in their insulated cocoons.

These inactive insects, in the stage of their life cycle most conducive to surviving the winter, spend the cold weather months in various places—in the leaf litter, in the bark of trees, inside dead or dying trees, in rotting logs, in the soil, attached to twigs, or in dark corners of buildings.

Although a beginning naturalist does not need to worry about identifying these inactive insects in winter, it is important to be aware of them for two reasons. First, their adaptations to winter represent efficient survival mechanisms. When their own food supply—plants, pollen, nectar, leaves, and other insects—disappears, so do they. Second, even though the insects themselves are inactive, they are still an important part of the winter food supply for the birds and other animals that remain active.

Birds that depend on insect food as a part of their winter diet include chickadees, nuthatches, and woodpeckers. Chickadees search twigs and outer branches for insects and insect eggs that might be hidden there. Nuthatches concentrate on the insects that have hidden themselves in the bark of tree trunks.

Downy and hairy woodpeckers dig deeper into the tree looking for woodboring insects. If you see a relatively large rectangular hole in a tree or branch, that's the work of another woodpecker, the pileated, which is searching for carpenter ants. These carpenter ants are among the most interesting insects of all. In experiments to determine just how they survive the freezing winter temperatures, researchers discovered that they manufacture a substance called *glycerol,* which is similar to the antifreeze we use in cars. Apparently, several species of ants and wasps produce glycerol for winter. When the temperature warms up again in the spring, the glycerol, which has kept the insects from freezing, disappears.

Birds are not the only animals looking for insect food in winter. Active mammals that need a lot of insects in their daily food supply to survive include shrews and moles. Both the masked shrew and the hairytail mole, for instance, have been known to eat up to three times their weight in food each day, mostly in insects. While birds are eating many of the insects that chose to hide in or on trees, shrews and moles are eating many of those which burrowed into the soil or thought they'd be safe in the leaf litter.

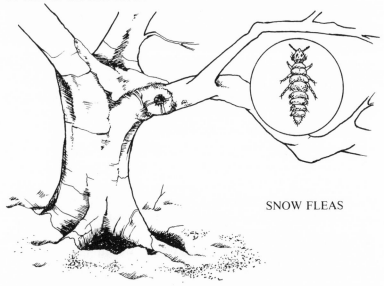

SNOW FLEAS

There is one live and active insect you may see during the winter if you're good at noticing very small things. It's called a snow flea, but it's not a flea at all. Real fleas are parasitic: they live on the blood of a host bird or mammal. The snow flea, on the other hand, eats microscopic bits of organic matter it finds in the snow.

If you're walking outdoors on a sunny winter day, look for these little black "fleas" on the surface of the snow. At first they look like spilled pepper. But then the specks of "pepper" begin to move. If you watch the snow fleas closely you will notice them leaping and jumping from place to place. They have a springlike structure for locomotion, which explains another name by which they are known—the springtail.

Another active insect that may pester you in the winter is one that sought a dark place inside your house when the cold weather came. When your furnace or fireplace warms your house, this particular insect, called the cluster fly, responds to the warmth by seeking light. Groups of them will "cluster" at your windows during the day, or if it's after dark they will fly into your lights.

While insects are important to birds and mammals in winter, they are even more important to everyone when the natural world reactivates in the spring. Mammals that supplement their summer diets with insects include mice, chipmunks, skunks, martens, foxes, raccoons, and bears. Returning birds eat many insects and feed many more to their young. Fish, reptiles, and amphibians also eat their fair share of insects. To this long list of hungry animals we must also add those insects which subsist on other insects that are smaller, slower, or less clever than themselves.

Without insects, many food chains would lose their most important links. Winter is a good time to begin learning about insects and the roles they play. Because they are not around to pester you, you can be more philosophical about their contributions to the natural world.

4

Winter Trees

One of my favorite sights in winter is the silhouette of a leafless tree against the evening sky. Every twig seems to show itself off in crisp detail, reminding us that a tree is not just trunk and branches but also an intricate system of growing tips.

In winter these growing tips are dormant, but they are not lifeless. They have already grown their buds, which contain next year's leaves and flowers. The buds are carefully packed and protected against the harsh winter weather, but they are alive and ready to open as soon as spring supplies the proper signals.

These buds are as revealing as leaves or bark or any of the other characteristics we might use to identify a tree. Each tree has distinctive buds arranged in distinctive ways. A study of twigs and dormant buds in winter will lead to a better understanding of the leafy, food-producing, growing trees of summer.

To understand how a twig is related to the rest of a tree, it is first necessary to understand how a tree grows. Many people, having watched only short-lived vegetables and flowers grow, might assume that a plant pushes up out of the ground and keeps on pushing up until it's reached the proper height. According to this theory, a tree, because it's a perennial, would go on pushing up year after year. If you made a mark close to the ground on the trunk of the tree, the mark should rise a little higher each year. But this is not the case.

If you've ever seen a piece of barbed wire from an old fence still attached to a living tree, you've probably noticed that it's still at fence height. It looks as if it has grown into the bark, however. This should give you one clue about one way a tree grows. The trunk and the branches grow fatter by one growth ring each year. The barbed wire has not grown into the tree; the growing tree has grown around the barbed wire.

If trees grew only fatter, however, we would have a lot of short fat trees. But we know that many trees grow quite tall. If the roots aren't pushing up more trunk from below, how do trees get so tall?

That's where the twigs come in. In addition to the thickening of the trunk and branches that goes on each year, there is some lengthening going on, too, but it's taking place only at the tips of the twigs and rootlets. We can't watch the rootlets grow because they're underground, reaching into the soil for the water and dissolved nutrients the tree needs to stay alive. But we can watch the twigs. They stretch the tree's leaves toward the sunlight they need to manufacture food.

A winter twig shows many things. It shows where last year's terminal bud was located. The bud scales that protected the terminal bud left a scar encircling the twig when they fell away. The distance from the bud scale scar to the new terminal bud shows how much growth occurred last summer. The new terminal bud will be responsible for next year's growth.

The twig also shows where the now fallen leaves were attached and even how the veins that transported nutrients and food into and out of the leaves were arranged. Finally, the twigs hold the buds that grew last summer but won't open until it's time for leaves and flowers in the spring.

With so much information available on winter twigs, it would be a shame to wait until the leaves come back to begin your study of trees. Gathering a twig collection from the trees near where you live can provide focus and direction for a winter walk. Then, identifying, comparing and contrasting, and studying the twigs indoors can take as long as you want it to.

Best of all, a study of winter twigs will make you more keenly aware of what is happening to the trees when changes are taking place too fast to watch them. I'm already looking forward to spring's unfolding of the tight little buds I've been watching since fall.

5

Woodpeckers

If you hang out a chunk of suet even late in the winter, you may be lucky enough to have some downy and hairy wood-peckers notice it. You will be able to learn quite a bit about woodpeckers from observing the behavior of these two com-mon species.

The downy woodpecker is supposed to be the more fre-quently seen of the two, but I seem to see the hairy more often. This winter I've seen a female hairy almost every day, feeding at the beef suet I've hung outside my kitchen window in a small onion bag. I've also noticed a male hairy exploring the trees out in front of my house for insects, but I've never seen him at the suet.

It's easy to tell the difference between a downy and hairy woodpecker if you see them close together or one right after the other. They are both black and white with almost identical pat-terns, but the hairy is quite a bit bigger than the downy.

If you see just one black and white woodpecker and wonder which one it is, compare the size of its beak to the size of its body. If the beak seems long, it's a hairy. If the beak seems pro-portional or even short, it's a downy. The hairy woodpecker is about the size of a robin, whereas the downy is about the size of a large house sparrow.

To tell the male from the female, look for a red patch on the back of the head. If a patch is there, the bird is a male. If it's not, the bird is a female. Woodpeckers are solitary in winter, so if you see one sex you won't necessarily see the other.

Woodpeckers, as their name implies, have a special relationship to wood. Many of their adaptations are connected to their lives as woodworkers. If you look at how a woodpecker positions itself on your suet or on a tree trunk, you can see how its body helps it work. It has strong feet that enable it to grasp and hang onto the bark of a tree.

WOODPECKER'S FOOT

Most birds have four toes arranged for perching, swimming, or walking. Three toes forward and one back seems to be a convenient arrangement for those activities. The woodpecker, however, has two toes forward and two back for maximum support and holding power. Three-toed woodpeckers are an exception. They have two toes pointing forward and only one to support them from behind.

When a woodpecker grasps the bark of a tree, it also presses its stiff tail feathers against the tree to provide additional support. When it begins its pecking, its body does not rock back and forth like a seesaw. Its feet and tail hold firm like a stable tripod, while its strong neck propels its head forward like a jackhammer.

The woodpecker's head is an amazing creation. Scientists

are studying it to see if they can borrow some ideas to improve the construction of crash helmets for human beings. The woodpecker is able to pound its beak against a hard object over and over again, and the percussion never addles its brain. Because human beings also seem bent upon knocking their heads against things, it's fortunate that researchers are designing "woodpecker helmets" to help us protect our vulnerable brains.

Another interesting feature of the woodpecker's head is its tongue. Instead of occupying only its mouth, two rear extensions reach beneath and behind the jaw, up the back of the skull, and over the top of the head. They are finally anchored in the woodpecker's right nostril.

WOODPECKER'S HYOID

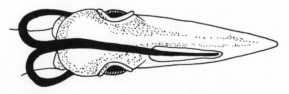

All this extra apparatus, which is called the hyoid, is necessary because the woodpecker needs to be able to stretch its tongue long distances to get at the grubs and insects it exposes. The tip of the tongue is pointed and has backward-slanting barbs, so with the help of the long, flexible hyoid the woodpecker can extend its specialized tongue and harpoon its insect food.

Trees are important to woodpeckers not only for providing insect food but also for providing homes. When it comes time for nesting, woodpeckers, in pairs, excavate a nice protected cavity for their eggs and young. In winter woodpeckers also have sleeping cavities that they either dig fresh or inherit from another woodpecker or another year's work.

You might think that all this excavating would be harmful to trees, but woodpeckers usually choose dead or dying trees or a live-looking tree with a dead heart. Their former nesting cavities (they dig a new one each year) and their winter shelters rarely become wasted space. Instead, they become good nesting places for birds that don't have the equipment to dig holes of their own. Bluebirds, wrens, flycatchers, and swallows are among the birds that may build their nests in old woodpecker holes. Flying squirrels and deer mice also like to set up housekeeping in leftover cavities.

All in all, woodpeckers are very beneficial birds. They do little harm to living trees, and if they do, as some claim sapsuckers do, they should be forgiven because they work so hard at controlling destructive insect pests.

When I walk in the woods behind my house I am glad to see that some of my trees are dead or dying. I call them my "woodpecker trees." The woodpeckers that will be attracted to them will eat insects and create homes for themselves and other animals. All the animals together will help maintain the balance between plant and animal life that keeps my woods a healthy place for everyone.

6

Snow

In New England we've been under snow long enough by February that it might be helpful psychologically to think about snow positively. One Vermonter who looked at snow positively—with almost religious awe—was "Snowflake" Bentley. Bentley began photographing snow crystals as a young man. In his lifetime he took over 5,000 individual photographs, using a camera and microscope that his parents bought him in 1885. Over 2,500 of his microphotographs were published in 1931, the year he died, in a book called *Snow Crystals.*

Bentley looked at each snowstorm as another opportunity to photograph snow crystals. Taking pictures of snow crystals isn't for everyone, but if we can share Bentley's fascination with individual snowflakes, as we look out the window at yet another snowstorm, perhaps we can enjoy rather than dread what we're going to have to live with anyway.

What Bentley's photographs teach you can learn yourself with a magnifying glass or hand lens. The next time it snows take a dark piece of fabric (some recommend velvet) or a board that you've painted black and catch the falling flakes against the dark background. A dark coat sleeve will also work. Look at the snowflakes through your magnifying glass, and you will see the delicate beauty that captivated Bentley.

You will begin to notice differences in the crystals if you look at a few in each new snow. All will have six sides, but beyond that basic similarity the variety is infinite. Bentley—and researchers since—have never found two identical crystals. Despite this infinite variety, meteorologists classify snow crystals into nine or ten basic types, each type reflecting the atmospheric conditions in which the crystal originated and through which it has passed on its descent to earth.

If you've just shoveled your walk or plowed your driveway, you're probably not in the mood to think about the beauty of individual snow crystals. But deep snow on the ground—even if we human beings have to keep digging and plowing our way out of it—has its advantages, too.

Perhaps snow's most significant contribution is to the plant kingdom. Once the snow comes to stay, all the roots and low-growing vegetation that have become dormant are insulated from the devastating temperature changes that occur throughout the winter. When the temperature is well below zero in the open air, it's usually just below zero near the surface of the snow and almost 32 °F. deep under the snow.

Snow insulates because it captures air as it settles to the ground, and all the little air pockets prevent warmth from escaping and cold from entering. On the forest floor, where the snow touches the earth, the temperature stays uniform throughout the winter. This unchanging temperature makes it possible for dormant plants, hibernating animals, and diapausal insects to survive weather that would be lethal if they were exposed to it.

Snow also stores moisture for the plant kingdom in the spring when seeds are ready to germinate and plants are ready to grow again. The moisture that doesn't evaporate from the surface of the snow during winter is stored in the frozen snow to provide the first spring watering when it begins to melt. Later, snow on the tops of mountains will melt and feed streams and rivers. And in some parts of the country this late-melting snow provides water for irrigation.

While dormant plants and hibernating animals benefit

from snow as insulation, active animals take advantage of it in other ways. Meadow mice, for instance, have whole networks of tunnels under the snow that enable them to move from food source to food source without exposing themselves to predators. In spring, when the snow is melting, I see the remains of these tunnels lacing the brushy fields near my house.

The star-nosed mole comes up from underground to dig tunnels through the bottom layer of snow in search of insects hiding in the leaf litter. The mole probably appreciates the ease of digging snow tunnels after three seasons of digging tunnels in the soil. The muskrat also digs snow tunnels that take it from food to water under the protection of snow.

The ruffed grouse doesn't go to the trouble of digging tunnels to take advantage of the snow's protection. On a cold winter night the grouse just dives right into a snowbank and settles into these insulated quarters. It leaves no tracks, and snow does not transmit odors, so the bird is well protected from predators.

Animals that live on top of the snow enjoy some advantages, too. Each new snow raises rabbits a little higher so that they can reach bark and twigs they couldn't get at before. Deer also benefit from a new snow that weighs down tree branches to bring untouched browse within their reach.

One last positive aspect of snow is winter recreation. Of course, wild animals don't play in the same way human beings do, but we, too, are a part of the natural world. The pleasure we find in moving across the surface of the snow should not be ignored.

By listing the positive things that snow does for plants, wild animals, and human beings, I do not mean to deny the very real hardships and inconveniences that it brings. I guess all I'm saying is that, since those of us who live in the North are going to have to live with snow almost half of every year anyway, we might as well learn to view it positively.

7

Groundhogs

Celebrating Groundhog Day on February 2 is a strange tradition. A groundhog—which is the same animal many people call a woodchuck—is supposed to emerge from its burrow to look at the weather. If it sees its shadow, we'll have six more weeks of winter. If it doesn't, we'll have an early spring. The only problem with this tradition is that the woodchucks that live in the part of the country where we worry about long winters are still hibernating on February 2.

The tradition has a long history. However, it's just that the woodchuck is not the right animal to cast in the role of weather prophet. In Europe the custom is to predict the arrival of spring on February 2, which is a church holiday, by watching for the shadow of a hedgehog or a badger. Neither of these animals is a hibernator, so it's not quite as farfetched to be looking for one or the other of them on February 2.

Although the woodchuck is a familiar animal, it is a frustrating one for a beginning naturalist to study because it goes by other common names—such as groundhog—and it is sometimes confused with other burrowing rodents such as the gopher and the prairie dog. Furthermore, as indicated by the mix-up between the animals involved in the European custom and the American Groundhog Day, the woodchuck has also been confused with the hedgehog and the badger.

The only animal that can be ruled out of this confusion immediately is the badger. Most of the others are rodents, which means gnawing mammals. They eat plant food. The badger is a carnivore, or meat eater, and a member of the same family that includes weasels, otters, and minks. The badger, in fact, eats rodents, which should help with the distinction.

The hedgehog is more troublesome because there are two different animals that are called hedgehogs. One is the Old World mammal that has hairs and spines somewhat like the porcupine's but is an insect eater rather than a plant-gnawing rodent. The other animal nicknamed "hedgehog" is the New World porcupine which is a rodent—but one that no one should confuse with the woodchuck.

To differentiate all these animals, it might help to turn to the standard classification system that gives all plants and animals internationally accepted Latin names. Full Latin classification includes:

Kingdom
Phylum
Class
Order
Family
Genus
Species

At each level of this classification system the animals that stay grouped together are more and more like each other in evolutionary history and physical adaptations. Finally, at the bottom of the classification system, at the species level, only animals that can interbreed are still in the same group.

At the top levels of this classification system woodchucks, badgers, Old World hedgehogs, New World porcupines, gophers, and prairie dogs are all grouped together. They all belong to the same kingdom (Animalia), phylum (Chordata), and class (Mammalia). At the level of order the badger and the Old World hedgehog are eliminated because of what they eat. The badger belongs to the order Carnivora (flesh eaters), and the Old World hedgehog belongs to the order Insectivora (insect eaters).

Among the remaining animals all belong to the order Rodentia (gnawing mammals), but porcupines and one group of gophers—the pocket gophers—are eliminated at the level of family. Porcupines belong to a family characterized by their sharp spines, or quills. The pocket gopher family is characterized by external, fur-line cheek pouches. The remaining gophers, which are also called ground squirrels, and the prairie dogs belong to the same family woodchucks belong to—the squirrel family. This family is characterized by daytime activity and hairy tails.

By the time we get to genus, the animals are quite similar, but they are still different in some aspects of behavior and appearance. Prairie dogs belong to one genus. They are smaller and more colonial than woodchucks, and they live in a different habitat—the prairies. Ground squirrels belong to another genus. They are quite a bit smaller than both prairie dogs and woodchucks. Some of them resemble chipmunks.

Finally, we have the woodchuck in a genus that excludes all the other animals that might be confused with it. This genus includes only the stout-bodied, short-legged, burrowing rodents called marmots. Within this genus, the woodchuck belongs to its own species, *monax.*

This brief lesson in taxonomy explains what the woodchuck, or *Marmota monax,* is and isn't, but not how it lives. Basically, the woodchuck is a daytime, plant-eating, burrowing rodent. It is active only during spring and summer, hibernating in its underground burrow throughout the winter.

The woodchuck emerges from hibernation sometime in the later winter or early spring—in my area, during maple sugaring. The male's first order of business is mating, and he will even dig through snowdrifts to find a burrow where a female of the species may be hiding. The young are born a little more than a lunar month after mating. They are naked, blind, and helpless at birth and remain inside the burrow for about five weeks.

During the spring and early summer the young stay with their mother, who watches them and sounds a shrill whistle of alarm if danger approaches. By midsummer the young woodchucks move out on their own, each one establishing a territory that will provide enough food to fatten it for the long winter's hibernation.

WOODCHUCK

Woodchucks eat only plant food. They do not supplement their diet with insects or other animal food. They spend their days eating and their nights sleeping, out of the way of nocturnal predators. The predator that harrasses woodchucks the most is the fox, but foxes should be understood as one of nature's necessary checks and balances. If foxes didn't eat a number of woodchucks every year, we would soon be overrun by them.

In addition to sleeping through nights and hibernating through winters, woodchucks have other survival strategies. Their burrows have several entrances and exits, which enable them to get into or out of the burrow fast, depending on the situation. The front entrance to the burrow can be told by the pile of dirt that's left after they've excavated. A back exit is usually hidden in brush or tall weeds. They also have a drop hole that provides the animals with a straight shot to safety when they need it. Woodchucks like to dig in open woods or in fields near the edge of woods. Deserted woodchuck burrows make good homes for other animals such as skunks and foxes.

On February 2, a self-respecting northern woodchuck is hibernating. It is underground, curled up in an almost lifeless ball. If you took a woodchuck out of its winter quarters on Groundhog Day, you could roll it around in the snow without disturbing its sleep. If you took it indoors, it would wake up slowly in response to the warmth, but you would have to wait a while before it started acting like a wide-awake woodchuck. Once you woke it up, I'm not sure what you'd do with it because it would probably be hungry and would soon want to mate.

Our desire to have the woodchuck come out of its burrow on February 2 to tell us what it knows about the weather is misguided. We should leave woodchucks alone until nature awakens them. Instead of wondering about the woodchuck's shadow while winter is obviously still with us, we should settle for seeing a woodchuck's tracks when spring is approaching.

8

Porcupines

While woodchucks, jumping mice, and some bats are hibernating and bears, chipmunks, raccoons, and skunks are dozing on and off, porcupines remain active throughout the winter. "Active," however, is not a very good word to describe the porcupine when you compare its "activities" with those of deer, squirrels, field mice, deer mice, rabbits, hares, and the active predators that prey on them.

Most of the animals that don't hibernate, sleep, or migrate to avoid harsh winter weather are hard pressed to stay alive. They are indeed active most of their waking hours searching for enough food to keep their bodies functioning. But there is no hurrying or chasing in a porcupine's life. Summer and winter it waddles. It is in no special rush about getting its food, nor does it need to race away from hungry predators.

One explanation for the porcupine's leisurely pace is the abundance of its winter food—the inner bark of trees. The porcupine is a rodent, or gnawing mammal. It uses its sharp, chisel-like front teeth to scrape away the outer bark of a food tree, exposing the tender, nutritious inner layer. It then gnaws at this inner bark until it's satisfied. It leaves large, maplike patterns of exposed wood where it has eaten away the bark. A porcupine sometimes works close to the ground where you can see its teeth marks. Sometimes it climbs high in a tree and gnaws interesting patterns in the bark up there.

I've seen evidence of a porcupine's past meals in beeches, maples, and white pines. It is also known to like hemlock, red spruce, balsam fir, and yellow birch. The porcupine doesn't have to worry that its food supply may run out before the winter ends. Nor does it have to grab up what food is available lest one of its competitors eat it first. There are lots of trees and not many animals competing for their bark, so the porcupine is pretty well set for its winter food.

PORCUPINE

As for predators, the porcupine has less to worry about than any other animal except the skunk. Both the porcupine and the skunk have unique defenses that have made them the successful animals they are. Actually, I think the porcupine is even better equipped than the skunk because its weapons can do permanent damage and even kill its attackers, whereas the skunk just makes predators wish they'd left well enough alone.

The porcupine's quills are an interesting evolutionary development. If you've seen a domestic cat bristle when it's angry, or if you've felt your own hair rise and tingle when you were in a tight spot, you've experienced a mild version of what the porcupine has refined to a high art. The porcupine's specialized quills are attached loosely to muscles in its skin. When the porcupine feels threatened, it turns its back to the enemy and raises its quills.

If that's not sufficient to scare the assailant off, the porcupine swings its clublike tail, catching the surprised predator across the snout and sinking a dozen or so quills into the sensitive area around the mouth and nose.

And that's not the end of the encounter. If the animal happens to be a domestic dog, it races home to its master, who will remove the quills or take the dog to a vet to have them removed. It's a painful process because the quills are barbed. Sometimes the only way to get them out is to pull a little flesh out with them.

If the animal is a creature of the wild, there is very little it can do. The tip of each quill is as sharp as a needle, so if the porcupine made a direct hit several quills will be stuck firmly into the animal's flesh. The warmth and moisture of the animal's flesh will raise thousands of microscopic, backward-slanting barbs. Any muscular action will cause the barbed quills to dig deeper.

Some of these unfortunate animals will die because a quill will work its way in and puncture a vital organ. Or the quills may be located so close to the mouth and jaw that the animal will not be able to eat, and will starve. The quills may also cause infection. One way or another, a porcupine can do considerable damage to its would-be predators.

Although the porcupine is well armored with about 30,000 quills, some parts of its body are vulnerable to attack: its face, throat, and stomach. Some animals are fast enough to get at these vulnerable places before the porcupine can use its weapons. The fisher is the best known of the porcupine's natural enemies, but bobcats, foxes, coyotes, and great horned owls have also enjoyed occasional successes.

Because porcupines find food easily and have an effective defense system, they have a good survival rate. Therefore, they don't have to produce as many offspring as some of their rodent cousins. Porcupines mate once a year in the fall, and the females bear one young in the spring. The gestation period lasts about seven months. The baby porcupines, which weigh about a pound at birth, are well developed.

The quills, of course, are soft when the baby is born, but they harden almost immediately. The baby's eyes are wide open from the beginning, and its teeth have already broken through its gums. Because porcupines are so advanced when they're born, they have only a short period of dependency. They are pretty much miniature adults from the time they enter the world.

I like to see porcupines or their wallowing, troughlike paths in the snow. I know there are at least two wintering in the woods near my house. Seeing them or signs of their presence reminds me that not all of nature's children are sleek, agile, keen-sighted, and swift. The porcupine's evolutionary path has allowed it to be slow, fat, nearsighted, and cumbersome— yet successful. The porcupine's success demonstrates that speed and power are not the only virtues in nature's complex rivalries. Species survive only if they have won—and continue to win—their rightful place among all the other evolving and competing life forms.

9

Beavers

While other active mammals can move around in search of food throughout the winter, beavers are trapped under several inches of ice. I begin to worry about the beavers that live at the foot of my hill as winter stretches on. When I walk across their frozen pond, I wonder just how they're doing under there.

Beavers don't hibernate. They store food for the winter by gathering branches in the fall and sticking them into the mud at the bottom of the pond. Some of these branches stick up above the surface of the water, which makes it look as if the beavers are accumulating a brush heap next to their lodge. The branches are frozen under or into the ice, and their bark is the beaver family's winter food supply.

Unlike other wild mammals, beavers stay together as a family during the winter. The beavers' winter food problem is therefore doubly complicated by the ice that limits them to only what they've managed to store in the fall and by the size of the family that has to share the limited food supply. The beaver family's situation is further complicated by the impending arrival of another litter. Once the ice melts the pressure is off, but a long thawless winter is especially threatening to beavers.

Beavers are unusual among wild mammals in that they keep two—and sometimes, for a brief period, three—generations of young with them simultaneously. The oldest brothers and sisters stay through the second mating season and then either leave or are driven out when they are ready to mate themselves. The yearlings stay a second season and help the parents with the new litter. Two to four young, called kits, are born each spring at the end of a 128-day gestation period.

The beaver family is somewhat like a human family with this pattern of older and younger offspring interacting with each other and depending on their parents for an extended period. Beavers are also like human beings in their ability to alter an environment to suit their purposes. Because they need water for protection and transportation, they build a dam across a brook or stream to create a pond. To extend their territory toward new food supplies, they build additional dams to create a waterway. They can swim through this waterway to the trees they want for food and for dam and lodge construction, floating heavy logs and branches to where they need them.

The first beaver dam I saw looked to me like a random assortment of sticks. Actually the construction was quite careful. Beavers cut logs to the length of five feet or so and then arrange them with the thick ends headed upstream. They weight these logs with rocks and mud and build up layer after layer until they have a dam that keeps the water level where they want it. Water is always trickling through, so the level of the pond stays relatively constant. In a time of heavy rains or rapidly melting snow, beaver dams help prevent floods. They hold the extra water and release it into swollen waterways slowly.

The beaver's home, or lodge, is another impressive engineering feat. It is built in the middle of the pond with its foundation under the water. The beaver wants water around its home for protection—it has neither the speed nor the equipment for a fight, so it needs water to protect it from hungry coyotes, bears, bobcats, and other large predators. And, since the entrance to the lodge is under water, the beaver limits its visitors to other aquatic species. The beaver family lives in a one-room apartment above water level. The mound of sticks you see in the middle of a beaver pond is the outside surface of the beaver's snug retreat.

Beavers are very efficient builders. They make maximum use of their building materials. First they chop down a tree of appropriate size and species. Favorites are small to medium-size aspens, willows, and yellow birches. One reason for cutting down a tree is to reach the tender bark of the upper twigs and branches—their preferred food. When the tree is down, the beavers cut it into manageable sizes and haul or float the pieces back to their lodge. After they've eaten the bark, they use bigger logs in construction and small sticks in combination with stones and mud for repair work.

Besides their engineering skills, beavers have a number of unusual adaptations that suit them for the kind of life they lead. They have a broad flat tail that helps them navigate in water. The tail functions as a rudder. It is also a warning device. A slap of the tail on the surface of the water is a signal to other beavers to dive.

The beaver also has webs between the toes of its hind feet to help it swim efficiently. Another set of special adaptations are transparent eyelids, valves that close the ears and nose when the beaver is under water, and loose lips that can close tightly behind the strong front teeth to enable the beaver to gnaw or carry branches under the water. The beaver also has a special tool for grooming—a cleft hind toe that functions as a comb for its thick, waterproof fur.

A beaver's front teeth are like other rodents' teeth except that they're bigger. They're designed for the special task of chopping down trees. All rodents eat by gnawing bark, twigs, and other forms of vegetation. The gnawing is necessary to keep the front incisors sharpened and worn down to proper length. If a rodent stops gnawing, its front teeth will grow until they reach a length that makes them useless to the animal, and the animal will eventually starve.

When a beaver cuts down a tree, the upper teeth dig into the tree and hold steady while the lower teeth cut a notch from below. The beaver removes the chip it's bitten, then bites again. Beavers have been known to fell a tree four inches thick in fifteen minutes.

Some people consider beavers an irritation and a nuisance. Foresters, for instance, resent the beavers' tree-cutting activities. Also, beaver ponds sometimes flood a wooded area and drown trees. Farmers and landowners, too, resent losing fields, pasture space, or lawns to beaver ponds.

People whose land use or livelihood is not threatened by a beaver pond might, on the other hand, be grateful for the beavers' arrival. A beaver pond creates a new and inviting habitat for all kinds of birds and wildlife. A pond brings with it new forms of vegetation, which are food for aquatic insects and animals. The small aquatic animals are in turn food for larger amphibians, reptiles, birds, and mammals. Dead trees provide cover for ducks and food for wood-boring insects, which are in turn food for woodpeckers. The woodpeckers' excavations become nest holes for wood ducks and other cavity-nesting birds. If, after a few years, the beavers exhaust the local food supply and move on, their unattended dam will fall into disrepair, and the pond will eventually drain to leave a flat, fertile meadow.

Whether you perceive beavers as friends or foes, they are an important part of the ecology wherever they live. Some things are lost when beavers move into a new neighborhood, but other things are gained. For those who are interested in the relationship between animals and their environments, beavers—with their unusual behavior and adaptations—are among the most fascinating of wild mammals to study and observe. I feel lucky to have a beaver family living within easy walking distance of my home. They are among my favorite neighbors.

10

Spiders

When we opened the sugarhouse to prepare for this year's sugaring, I saw a tangle of spiderwebs in the light coming in through the door. As I looked around I discovered more spiderwebs in corners, between beams, even in the evaporating pans. I thought back to when we had scrubbed all the equipment and locked the house securely for the three seasons before we would sugar again. The dark, untenanted building had been visited by no vandals, but it had obviously been a busy place for spiders.

A spider's web is its universe. Web-spinning spiders don't like to move around because they don't see very well, so they build their world around themselves. The delicate strands of the web are compensation for the sensory equipment they lack. What they can't see they feel. One kind of vibration means a meal has just arrived. Another kind advises the female that an interested male is about to pay a call.

The web is also a trap. Spiders prey on insects, and a web is perfect for catching them. Once the insect hits the web, its life is in danger. If the web is sticky, the insect becomes stuck in the silk, and its very struggle to free itself is an invitation to the spider to come directly to where the trapped insect is making its commotion. If the web isn't sticky, the spider has to chase the insect, but since the spider has the advantage of being on its home turf it usually wins the chase.

Because the spider likes its food alive, it doesn't kill the insect immediately. It injects it with a paralyzing venom. Some spiders even wrap the insect in silk for temporary storage. A spider doesn't have teeth, so when it's ready to eat, it injects the paralyzed insect with a digestive fluid that turns the insect to liquid. Finally, the spider's stomach starts pumping and sucking, and the spider eats its meal of paralyzed, liquefied insect.

The webs I saw in the sugarhouse were of three different kinds. The one that first attracted my attention was a large tangled cobweb that seemed to go every which way. This web was probably the work of a comb-footed spider. These spiders have combs on their hind legs that help them throw liquid silk over trapped insects. Among their favorite places to build cobwebs are the upper corners of cellars, attics, barns, and sugarhouses. These spiders weave their irregular webs and then wait for their prey to get caught in a sticky globule of wet silk. The spider waits in a closely woven part of the web, hanging with its back downward. When an insect gets stuck in the web, the spider moves in the direction of the vibration. The spider then throws liquid silk over the insect and eats it when it's hungry.

While I was studying the huge irregular cobweb, I noticed a more symmetrical orb web just below it. Half of the beautiful web had been torn away, but I could still see the intricacy and detail that distinguish this web from other types. The orb-weavers are the spiders that get the most attention from photographers and poets. Their webs are indeed works of art.

The orb weaver builds its web after dark. It begins by throwing out a thread to form a bridge between two points. Once this bridge has been established, the spider goes back and forth across it to reinforce it with more silk. When the bridge is secure, the spider drops straight down from the middle of the bridge on a thread it has attached to one strand of the bridge. When it finds a place to secure its vertical line, it pulls the one bridge strand down to a point about halfway between the bridge and the place where it will secure the vertical line. The web now looks like an upside-down triangle with a string pulling at its apex. The apex is the center of what will become the orb web.

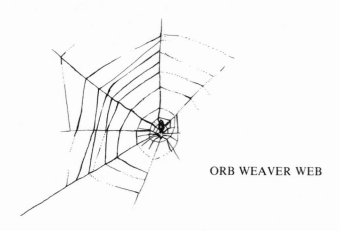

ORB WEAVER WEB

After the spider has secured the vertical thread, it returns to the center of the web and begins to build the radii. Each radius, or spoke, has to be attached at the hub of the web and to a bridge or some fixed point offered by the plants, beams, walls, or window frame to which the orb weaver is attaching its web. After the bridges and spokes are complete, the spider still has to walk in a carefully spaced spiral around the hub to create the final strands of the web. First, it builds a temporary spiral starting at the hub and working outward. Then it reverses its direction and builds a more substantial spiral as it retraces its steps back toward the hub. The strands of this spiral are covered with sticky silk to catch the spider's prey.

The last type of web I noticed looked almost like a piece of fabric. It was a thick flat web that had collected a lot of dust. This web was probably woven by one of the indoor relatives of the funnel weavers, or grass spiders. A funnel weaver is characterized by a pair of exceptionally long spinnerets. When it builds its sheetlike web it first uses a pair of its ordinary-length spinnerets to build a series of strong parallel threads. The spider then crisscrosses these threads in all directions with finer threads from its long spinnerets. The web itself isn't sticky, but once the spider feels an insect's presence it rushes after its prey and usually catches it.

A number of spiders have probably led happy lives in the peace and quiet of the unused sugarhouse. But now that it's time for sugaring again, the webs will have to be swept aside. If any spiders or their eggs are destroyed during this housecleaning, it is unfortunate because spiders are among the best insect controls one could ask for. Once we've finished with sugaring, we will move out of their way, and they can have the whole sugarhouse to themselves until it's time to sugar again next year.

11

Maple Sap

Chances are that if you hear the word "tap" or "tapping" at this time of year the people you're listening to aren't talking about dancing. A "tapping bit" is a 7/16-inch drill bit. To "tap" means to drill a hole about three inches into a maple tree and drive in a metal (or plastic) spout.

Although sugaring time comes every year just as predictably as winter or spring, it doesn't begin with a solstice or an equinox or even a specific date on the calendar. It begins sometime in late February or early March when the weather strikes a balance between the changing seasons. When it's cold at night and warm during the day, sap starts moving in the vessels inside a tree. That's when we tap our maple trees to take some of their sweet sap for our syrup-making operations.

The big mystery to sugar makers and scientists alike is what makes the sap move at this time of year. The current theory, and there have been many, is that when the temperature rises above 32° F. maple sap expels carbon dioxide. This carbon dioxide forms bubbles that collect in the fibers surrounding the sap vessels. The expanding carbon dioxide squeezes the vessels and puts pressure on the sap inside. This pressure forces the sap upward and downward toward the points of least resistance.

A taphole creates an unexpected point of low resistance when it severs the vessels. Some of the sap that would have been pushed upward or downward by the pressure of expanding carbon dioxide is diverted right out the spout into the waiting sap bucket. Although sap moves up and down in the sap-conducting vessels, there is no significant lateral movement unless a taphole intrudes. Two tapholes in the same tree are completely independent of one another because each has severed a different group of vertical vessels.

If the weather stays warm for a while, sap stops running. Without a return of cold weather, the taphole will run dry and stay dry. The return of cold weather, however, allows the tree to recharge itself. The carbon dioxide contracts and reenters the sap solution. More water is drawn up into the sap-conducting vessels through the root system. When the temperature rises again the carbon dioxide expands and exerts pressure on the sap, and more sap moves up and down the tree and out the taphole.

Although this explanation is based on controlled scientific experiments and observations, it is still only theory. New research at Harvard Forest is already suggesting revisions. To those of us who merely like maple syrup, the exact "why" of sap flow is unimportant. I'm just glad the Indians discovered that it happens—and that they shared the sweet substance they made from maple sap with my ancestors. The maple syrup we boil at this time each year is a perfect way to celebrate the end of winter and the beginning of spring.

12

Redpolls

Redpolls are easy to recognize. They are small, streaked, sparrowlike birds with red head patches. Both male and female have this red head patch, and both have a black patch under their bills, too. The male has additional red coloring on his chest. In spring the red coloring becomes brighter. Redpolls molt just once in the fall and grow new feathers with grayish fringes that mute and subdue the red patches. As winter goes by, the fringes wear away, and the red again becomes more prominent. On a clear sunny day in late winter the redpoll's red cap glistens brilliantly. As if to announce the approaching mating season, the male's chest also becomes redder and redder.

The only bird that a beginning birder might confuse with a redpoll is the male purple finch. The purple finch, however, is bigger and has more red coloring. His entire head is reddish, as are much of his chest and back all the way down to his tail. A male purple finch looks as if someone poured raspberry topping over his head.

Redpolls come south in winter in search of food. Some winters they apparently find enough food north of New England, for no one sees them this far south. Other winters they may be seen in New England, but not in the same places they were seen the prior winter or may be seen the next. Redpolls tend to visit different areas different winters, and they also move around from place to place while they're here. They eat the weed seeds they find in brushy fields or congregate at feeders that offer mixed seed.

The National Audubon Society's Annual Christmas Bird Counts help indicate whether it's a "redpoll winter" or not. For example, the 1977 Burlington, Vermont count included 133 common redpolls. In 1976, however, no redpolls were spotted. In 1975 there were 196, but in 1974 there were none. Redpoll migrations are not cyclic, as these figures might imply. Their visits to New England or to a particular part of New England are merely irregular.

REDPOLL

This year a flock of redpolls showed up at my feeder in mid-February. I don't know where they were before they arrived, but they have apparently decided to spend the rest of their time in this area with me. They visit my seed tray and eat the mixed seed I scatter for them every day. I am watching them closely for signs of their leaving. Shortly they will head north to nest in the rugged and stunted trees near the edge of the arctic tundra.

If you see one redpoll, you'll probably see many others. They travel in flocks, sometimes with as many as fifty or more birds moving around together. My flock of redpolls seems to consist of twenty to twenty-five individuals, but it's difficult to count them because they are restless little creatures and don't stay still for long at a time.

The redpolls were attracted to my feeder by the hemp, millet, and sunflower seeds in the mixed seed I offer them. In the wild they feed primarily on ragweed seeds. They also like the seeds of birches and alder. When they're nesting, redpolls eat insects and feed them to their young, but during winter they are almost exclusively vegetarian.

Redpolls are friendly and not especially afraid of human beings. At one time people caught these unwary creatures and kept them as pets, but now, fortunately for the redpolls, it is illegal to keep a wild bird in a cage. Redpolls are also frequent victims of house cats because they visit feeders in neighborhoods where house cats live and don't seem to recognize them as predators. In the wild a redpoll's enemies are uncatlike. They include owls, hawks, and shrikes.

I am enjoying watching my late winter redpolls closely each day to see if they will give me any signs of their leaving. When they do, I'll wish them well on their return to the rigors and solitude of the arctic tundra.

13

Pussy Willows

The spring equinox is that invisible time of year when everything is happening but nothing shows. Shortly the pastels and greens of buds, flowers, and leaves will tint the wooded hillsides. Migrating birds will return, and the earliest wild flowers will appear on the forest floor. As I look out my window on an overcast March day, however, it seems that winter has managed to kill off just about everything this year. These transitional days are a good time to look for quiet reassurances—like pussy willows.

Pussy willows need no introduction. Even in this era of television and "indoor insights," most people are familiar with the pussy willow. They may have even rubbed one against their cheeks, around their lips, or under their ears. The pussy willow invites this intimacy, even if giving human beings pleasure is not its primary purpose.

Pussy willows are the male portion of the willow tree's reproductive system. Shortly, the smooth, silver "pussies" will open into yellow, pollen-laden catkins. In willow trees male catkins grow on one tree, and different-looking female catkins grow on another. But nature has made perfect plans to see that the male pollen will reach the female catkins so that willow trees can reproduce their kind.

When bees first start looking for food in the spring, they head straight for the willow trees because willows are among the earliest pollen and nectar producers. The hungry bees gather some pollen from the male trees and then visit the female trees for nectar. The bees pollinate the willows unwittingly while they themselves are gathering food.

If you'd like to watch the silver-gray bud of the pussy willow turn into a pollen-bearing catkin, you can bring a twig indoors and put it in a glass of water. Willow twigs are amazingly adaptable. A twig in water will eventually root, and if it's returned to moist soil it will grow into a new willow tree. A twig can produce a new willow more rapidly than a willow seed that has to start from scratch.

BUDS OF PUSSY WILLOW

The best place to look for pussy willows is along the banks of a stream, near wet ditches, around the edges of a pond or marsh, or anywhere the ground stays wet. Willows provide an important service to the wet soil they grow in. Their roots are thick, fibrous masses that hold onto soil during floods and periods of high water.

Willows are a large and varied group of trees, including more than 100 species in North America. The weeping willow, a cousin of the pussy willow, is a native of China, but it has been planted so widely throughout the world that it is as familiar to most of us as the pussy willow. In addition to having so many different species, willows also have the ability to interbreed, making identification difficult even for experienced botanists.

All willows have male or female catkins, but there's only one species that has the soft silver buds that we think of as pussy willows. It's a shrubby tree with a short trunk and lots of branches, sometimes growing twenty to twenty-five feet tall. The pussy willow's Latin name is *Salix discolor.* It grows throughout the Northeast and as far south as Delaware, Maryland, and Missouri.

Salix discolor may be just another shrubby willow during most of the year, but in early spring its familiar buds are a promise of returning life. They offer us a little hint of this year's color amidst the browns and grays of last year's life.

Spring into Summer

14

Foxes

On a recent walk home from the sugar bush I caught a whiff of what I thought was a skunk. When I started looking around to locate the source of the odor, however, I discovered a fox den. A male fox marks his territory with a scent that smells very much like skunk, although I'm sure human beings are the only animals confused by the apparent similarity.

These foxes have located themselves in prime food-getting territory. Their den is on a hillside near the edge of a thick stand of white pines. Nearby are brushy fields. In the snow not far from the den I saw tracks of a deer mouse, a snowshoe hare, and a ruffed grouse. The melting snow in the neighboring fields is riddled with tunnels made by meadow mice. Any one of these animals is a potential meal or snack for a hungry fox.

Just outside the entrance to the underground den I noticed the feathers of a ruffed grouse—perhaps the same one that had made the nearby tracks. The male fox must have brought the grouse home to share with his mate. If she has already given birth to their young, she is trapped at home with them. If she has not given birth, she is at least in the advanced stages of her pregnancy.

Foxes are among the earliest of the spring maters. The male starts his search for a vixen—possibly the same female he consorted with the previous year—in late January or early February. By March the pair is well settled into domestic routines. The vixen's gestation takes about fifty-one days, so a pair that has mated by the first of February may be ready to have their litter by the third or fourth week in March. By the third or fourth week in April the pups will be mature enough to come out of the den.

Fox pups are born furred, but their eyes stay closed for over a week. There are usually about four or five of them in a litter. The vixen stays with them at first, and the father fox brings her food. When the babies are ready for solid food, both parents hunt and bring what they find back to the young. The pups are weaned when they are eight to ten weeks old, but the family stays together for the entire summer while the parents teach the young to hunt. In the fall the fox family breaks up, and each individual establishes his or her own territory for winter food gathering.

Foxes and dogs belong to the same family and have similar characteristics. Their footprints show four toes with toenail marks, but the tracks left by a fox are tidier than those left by a domestic dog. Droppings are also similar, although differences in texture and content would probably be revealed by close inspection because the domestic dog eats dog food and the fox eats what it can find.

In the eastern United States there are two types of foxes: the red fox and the gray fox. The den I've discovered belongs to a red fox. The gray prefers rocky, ledgy areas and usually dens in a hollow log or tree or in a crevice among rocks. The gray fox is rarely seen because it is a nocturnal hunter. Interestingly enough, the gray fox is also a tree climber—something that is quite unusual for a member of the dog family.

I have seen several red foxes—or their tracks—in my neighborhood at different times of the year. One was ambling across an open field on a sunny summer day. Several have run across the road in front of my car. Whenever I go animal tracking in the winter, I see the straight-line tracks a fox leaves when it's searching the woods and fields for food.

This year I look forward to watching a whole fox family in action. I know that foxes are quick to change dens if they are disturbed, so I will have to visit them quietly and resist impulses to approach too close to the den. Watching animals in the wild requires a discipline not necessary at zoos. But the rewards of seeing animals leading natural lives in natural habitats are so great that the discipline is worth it.

15

Edible Wild Foods

Every year in early spring wild food enthusiasts welcome back the earliest edibles. It's a good feeling to know that greens can come from woods and fields now instead of from the freezer.

Nature offers a number of treats to the person willing to study plants. But the plant kingdom also holds some dangers for the "instant expert." Our ancestors must have done a lot of testing over a long period of time before they discovered what was edible and what was not from among the plants around them. It therefore seems the height of romantic folly to fling ourselves upon nature and expect the plant kingdom to nourish us gently just because we've decided to notice it again.

Plants are not evil. The ones that are poisonous do not harm us and other animals because they have some ill will toward the animal kingdom. Plants merely live in accordance with their adaptations. Because it is we who come to them, it is our responsibility to learn about them before we eat them.

The study of edible wild foods is complicated by folklore, differing common names, and plant look-alikes. Even culti-vated foods are surrounded by myths, differences of opinion, and unpredictable happenings such as allergic reactions. If we look at some known facts about familiar plant foods, perhaps we can approach wild foods with a healthier attitude.

Some cultivated plants are safe to eat only at certain stages of their growth. "Plain old" potatoes, for instance, are toxic before they have matured. Their sprouts are toxic at any time—they contain solanine, a strong poison.

Other garden vegetables are edible either young or old, but the plants they grow on produce a combination of edible and toxic parts. The tomato plant, which was considered wholly poisonous until relatively recently, produces an edible fruit (the tomato itself, green or red) but poisonous leaves. Rhubarb also offers both edible and poisonous parts—the leaf stalks are edible, but the leaf blades are poisonous.

Still other plants need to be prepared in one way and not another if they are to be safe. Tobacco can be dried and smoked, but its leaves are toxic if cooked as greens. In studying edible wild plants, therefore, we must learn more than just their names. We must also learn at what stage in their life cycle they are edible, what parts of them are edible, and how to prepare them.

Another problem with wild foods involves common names. Socrates, for instance, killed himself with "hemlock," but American Indians brewed a "hemlock" tea to prevent scurvy. Socrates' hemlock was *Conium maculatum,* a native of Eurasia. It grows in marshy areas, ditches, and waste places throughout the United States. Its common name is poison hemlock, it belongs to the parsley family, and it looks a little like Queen Anne's lace. The Indians' hemlock tea, on the other hand, was boiled from the evergreen needles of the harmless hemlock tree, *Tsuga canadensis.*

A more dangerous confusion may be caused by a poisonous plant with a common name that is also used for an edible plant. Skunk cabbage, for instance, is edible, and some wild foods cookbooks include recipes for skunk cabbage dishes. But these recipes are for *Symplocarpus foetidus,* which when crushed smells like a skunk. Many people in Vermont and the rest of New England call a different plant "skunk cabbage" and therefore might decide to eat it on the basis of a wild food recipe. This plant is actually *Veratrum viride,* or false hellebore. False hellebore contains alkaloids that reduce blood pressure to a dangerous, possibly lethal, level.

FALSE HELLEBORE

New Englanders who have poisoned themselves by eating what they called "skunk cabbage" were not necessarily bad botanists. Perhaps even the naturalists in their neighborhood called the same plant "skunk cabbage," so they were victims of confusing language rather than of ignorance or irresponsibility.

Finally comes the problem of plant identification. If you think you've found a plant that is perfectly safe and edible and it turns out to be a deadly look-alike, you're in trouble. Probably most mushroom poisonings—those which aren't totally irresponsible—result from faulty identifications of look-alikes.

False hellebore has caused some problems in this respect, too. I heard the story of a person who brought friends some "wild leeks" to enjoy for dinner. The friends cooked up the greens and ate enough of them to find themselves seriously ill because their "leeks" were actually the young leaves of false hellebore.

The confusion in this case was probably visual. Both leeks and false hellebore are early spring arrivals. Both have pointed oval leaves that are ribbed lengthwise, but hellebore has leaves with much more definite ribs. Perhaps to a beginner fresh young hellebore leaves, which do look quite delicious, might look like wild leek leaves, but they could not possibly smell like them. Leeks smell strongly of onions, whereas false hellebore has no distinguishing smell.

I certainly do not intend to discourage the eating of wild foods. If anything, I would encourage people to return as much as possible to the natural foods available in their environment. Doing so would make better—and better fed—naturalists out of them. What I am warning against is the kind of "instant expertise" that twentieth-century Americans have come to desire and assume. If this instant expertise involves only equipment, "gismos," and opinions it's harmless enough, but as an attitude toward nature it's inappropriate and dangerous. You have no consumer rights or guarantees when you choose to eat wild food. You have only the responsibility to respect plants and learn about them before you commit the very significant act of eating them.

16

The Frog Run

Frogs herald the end of maple sugaring. The first sleighbell sounds of spring peepers coincide with the budding of the maple trees. When the trees begin to bud the sap begins to taste less sweet, and the sugaring season is over for another year.

Who are these little peepers that announce the final run of good-tasting sap? They are almost invisibly small amphibians that inhabit woodland ponds and wet areas near woods. A peeper is difficult to see because it is only about an inch long, it is well camouflaged by its dark color, and it tends to signal its presence only after dark. The peeper's Latin name is *Hyla crucifer.* The "crucifer" refers to a cross—actually more of an X—on its back.

Early in the spring peepers emerge from beneath moss or leaf litter where they've been hibernating all winter and seek a wet place where they can mate. Their high-pitched call, which begins late in the afternoon, is a mating song. Only the male sings. He is announcing his presence and inviting females to visit him to have their eggs fertilized.

If you go looking for peepers after dark, you may see one with the help of a flashlight. The male's white vocal sac swells up when he sings, so you may be able to spot the white area and find the frog that way.

A frog that emerges even earlier than the peeper in some neighborhoods is the wood frog. Wood frogs are so anxious to mate that they may settle for a pond that still has a skin of ice on it. As soon as the males find a pond, they begin to make a racket.

The first time I heard a chorus of wood frogs I thought my neighborhood had been invaded by a flock of nervous ducks. When I got closer to the commotion, however, I saw no ducks. The quacking was the love cries of numerous small wood frogs. The wood frog is easier to find than the peeper because it's bigger and it sings in broad daylight. Its dark robber's mask stretching back from its eyes makes it easy to identify.

Wood frogs and peepers are the earliest spring singers, but as the days become longer and warmer others will appear. Frogs and toads are a group of animals that the beginning naturalist can master without much difficulty. In my own area, only seven types of frogs and one type of toad are commonly seen. Whatever species are native to your area, early spring is the best time to start learning about these amphibians because their mating songs will lead you right to them.

The peeper is a tree frog, one of Vermont's two species of tree frogs. A sticky disc on each toe enables tree frogs to climb. The other tree frog is the gray tree frog, whose Latin name is *Hyla versicolor*. The "versicolor" refers to this frog's ability to change color to match its background. I once saw one that was a shiny green to match the leaf it was sitting on.

Because the color of the gray tree frog is dependent on where you find it, identification can be difficult. One sure way to recognize it, however, is to observe the light spot beneath its eye. The gray tree frog is bigger than the peeper and mates later. Its love song is a short, loud trill. Although both tree frogs prefer trees to ponds, they have to return to water to mate. Look for them near water at this time of year.

In addition to the two tree frogs, Vermont has five frog species that do not live in trees. They are called true frogs.

The early-singing wood frogs are among these true frogs. Their clamorous singing makes them easy to find. After only a few days of mating, however, the wood frogs will discontinue their songs, and both males and females will move away from their ponds into the woods. If you miss them while the males are singing, you can look for their robber's masks later in the spring and summer when you're walking in the woods.

BULLFROG

Vermont's other true frogs are the leopard frog, the pickerel frog, the green frog, and the bullfrog. The leopard frog, another early singer, is probably the most common frog in the United States. Your chances of seeing it somewhere—if not in the wild, perhaps in a biology laboratory—are pretty good. Leopard frogs are sometimes called "meadow frogs" because after they've mated they wander away from ponds into nearby meadows. They are predominantly green with round, dark spots like a leopard's. The spots are rimmed with white. The only frog you might confuse with the leopard frog is the pickerel frog, but the pickerel frog's spots are square or rectangular and are arranged in two parallel rows down its back. Both leopard and pickerel frogs snore when they sing, but the leopard frog adds what can best be described as a few extra grunts.

The green frog and the bullfrog stay closer to their ponds than the other frogs. They are both green to greenish brown and have dark blotches on their backs. They look very much alike, but the green frog has folds along the sides of its back, and the bullfrog doesn't. Also the male green frog has a bright yellow throat, whereas the bullfrog's is a paler yellow. The green frog's love song sounds like someone plunking on a loose banjo string. The bullfrog's song is the famous "jug-a-rum."

Vermont has only one commonly seen toad. A toad is not a frog, and it does not give you warts. Frogs have smooth, moist skin, whereas toads are dry and covered with the warts that have earned them their bad reputation. Although the warts are not contagious, handling a toad is still a somewhat unpleasant business. To defend itself from predators, it secretes a substance from its skin glands that irritates mucus membranes.

Toads are basically uglier than frogs. In addition to their warts, they have broad, chunky bodies. They are also quite awkward. Their hind legs are designed for hopping, while frogs' are designed for leaping and swimming. As if to compensate the toad for its unattractiveness, nature has given it a beautiful song—a high, flutelike trill. Once you learn to distinguish a toad from a frog, you should have no trouble identifying the American toad. Look for it in your garden later in the spring and summer, and consider it a friend because it eats insects by the hundreds.

The warm sunny days of spring will shortly invite all the frogs and toads out of hibernation to attend to the important business of mating. Listen for their love songs, and when you hear one try to find the singer and identify him. Frog watching is a good preoccupation during these transitional weeks when it's too late for sugaring and too early for planting. While you're listening and looking, you'll be bound to notice other early signs of spring. It won't be long now before the whole natural world is back in action.

17

Robins

The robin is the traditional symbol of spring. Some years I begin to wonder whether we're ever going to have a spring, but the robin's reappearance always gives me hope. The first to come back are the males. Researchers who have followed the males' progress northward have determined that the migration coincides with rising temperatures. The males arrive in an area when the average daily temperature has reached about 35–37° F. Whatever seasonal signals bring the advance guard back each spring, I'm certainly glad to see them when they arrive.

The early males will establish territories where they intend to nest. Robins like open woodland and forest edges. They also seem to enjoy the habitats human beings create around their homes. It is almost as if robins have chosen to accept and associate with us, while other species have withdrawn to whatever wilderness is left, as farms, suburbs, and cities have taken up more and more space.

Shortly after the earliest males arrive the females begin to appear. Robins return to the same territory year after year, and they sometimes choose the same mates. They do, however, build a new nest each year. For a building site they usually select a fork on a horizontal branch. Sometimes they build on a windowsill, ledge, or beam of a house or outbuilding.

The nest is built almost entirely by the female. The male helps out by bringing her grass, weed stems, strips of cloth, and bits of string. The outside of the nest looks loose and straggly, but the inside is smooth and finished. The female lines it with mud and soft grasses to make a strong, compact, and comfortable place to lay her eggs. While the mud is still damp she shapes the interior to fit the contours of her body.

She usually lays four eggs, which are the familiar turquoise-blue color we refer to as "robin's egg blue." She incubates them, with perhaps a little help from the male, for eleven to fourteen days. After the eggs hatch the busy days of feeding the young begin. The baby birds stay in the nest for about fourteen to sixteen days, and they have to be fed great quantities of insects, caterpillars, and earthworms during this period. Their small bodies are growing, and they need a lot of protein during this stage. Later, as adults, they will switch to a diet more evenly balanced between plant and animal food—usually about 60 percent fruits and other plant parts and 40 percent insects and earthworms.

When the first brood leaves the nest the male parent continues to attend them, while the female prepares herself for another brood. She either tidies up the old nest or builds a new one. For about two weeks the male teaches the first brood how to find and catch their own food. By the time the firstborn are ready to care for themselves, the second brood is ready to hatch, and the male and his mate have the awesome task of feeding another set of babies. Robins do not toil needlessly, however. About 80 percent of the young die during their first year, so adult robins have to produce a lot of young to maintain a healthy population.

As a species robins have adapted well to the changes human beings have made in the natural world. We are fortunate to have a companion species that sings to us so cheerfully as we say good-bye to winter and turn our attention toward the chores of spring.

18

Wood Ducks

The male wood duck is perhaps the most beautiful bird in North America. His special beauty lies in his combination of lines and colors. White streaks divide his head and body into carefully delineated sections. A vertical white stripe on his sides divides his bronze chest from his buffy hindparts. His white throat divides his head from his neck. A white streak running back from his eye draws attention to his iridescent crest. Another pair of white lines, one coming up from his throat and one stretching back from his bill, set off his orange-red eye.

The white streaks and sections of color, some of them metallic or iridescent, create the impression of a mechanical bird, a robot beauty from another world. The wood duck's mate, a more ordinary-looking brownish bird, has bold white eye rings, which make her look as if she is staring wide-eyed at the male's beauty. The wood ducks' Latin name, *Alix sponsa,* means "the betrothed," comparing the male's magnificent plumage to wedding attire.

The wood duck's courtship consists of a simple display of his crest. The male swims close to a desired female and perhaps touches her with his bill. Then he raises and lowers his head, showing her his crest. He makes soft guttural sounds to announce his interest.

If the female accepts him as her mate, she takes over and leads him everywhere he goes until she begins incubating her eggs. At that point the male joins up with other males, and they hide themselves away to molt. They lose their brilliant feathers, and for much of the summer they look like the more subdued females. This temporary stage is called their "eclipse." In molting all their primary wing feathers drop at once, so in addition to losing their beauty, they lose the ability to fly. Summer must be a humiliating time for these regal birds. In the fall, however, they molt again and regain their full color in advance preparation for the following spring.

The female, meanwhile, spends the summer raising her young. She incubates her eggs for about thirty days. When the ducklings hatch from the eggs they are covered with down and ready to leave the nest almost immediately. Sharp little claws on their toes enable them to climb out of the cavity in which their mother has chosen to nest. Once they reach the exit, though, they have a problem. They are equipped to walk and swim, but they can't fly. Their only means of getting to the ground and thence to water is to jump, and sometimes their mother has been inconsiderate enough to nest high in a tree. The baby ducklings are mostly air and fluff, however, and plunges from as high as fifty or sixty feet apparently do them little damage. After landing with a bounce they find their feet and parade behind their mother to water.

Watching a mother wood duck with her ducklings is great entertainment. The small ducklings are all motion and curiosity. They paddle around the pond, moving at top speed in all directions. The mother, who floats serenely nearby, will occasionally call them back, and they will gather around her for a few seconds before they start venturing off again.

Ducklings are very vulnerable because they can't fly, and they are so small that they can be gobbled up by predators that would be no threat to an adult—bullfrogs, for instance. The mother does her best to protect all of them, but the size of her brood is the only real protection for the species.

The female wood duck molts just once, toward the end of summer, and she, too, is temporarily flightless. Then comes the fall migration. Wood ducks leave fairly early and don't migrate very far. During the winter males and females mingle together, apparently indifferent to each other's sex. But come spring the courtships will begin again, and once the female has selected her mate she will lead him north to nest. Female wood ducks—both adults and year-olds—are likely to return to the neighborhood where they were born. The males, however, are freewheelers; they follow the female they mate with each spring to her pond.

Wood ducks, as the name indicates, like woodland ponds. They spend some of their time out of water, sunning themselves, preening on tree stumps, or perching in trees. They wander into the woods in search of nuts and fruits. Their powerful gizzards enable them to digest acorns, beechnuts, and other hard seeds. They also eat the leaves of aquatic vegetation such as duckweed. A small portion of their diet is animal food, and they show some preference for spiders.

Early in this century wood ducks were an endangered species. Their beauty made them vulnerable to collectors and feather hunters. Their tendency to nest near human habitations and their willingness to visit decoys made them vulnerable to hunters. But perhaps the greatest threat to their survival was the loss of nesting sites. Because they need cavities in trees near a pond or swamp, the cutting of trees and the draining of wetlands deprived them of places to nest. The combination of restrictive hunting laws and the preservation of wetlands has restored their populations to healthier proportions.

Wood ducks return to the North each spring shortly after the local frogs begin to sing. They don't advertise their presence with as much noise as frogs, but their beauty, once you've seen it, will invite you back to their woodland pond again and again. You must learn to be quiet and motionless, to see wood ducks, but one glimpse of the regal male will make you feel that way anyhow. I can think of no better initiation to the pleasures of birdwatching than seeing a male wood duck in full plumage.

19

Woodcocks

Certain sounds are a sure sign that spring is here. One is the strange little "peent" of the woodcock. The woodcock's peent may not be as beautiful as other birds' love songs, but the male's courtship behavior rivals the performances of even the most demonstrative suitors.

WOODCOCK

The first time I listened for woodcocks I had only read about them in books, and I had no idea what the nasal "peent" sounded like. It was late spring, and there were numerous other sounds to confuse me. I kept listening for something that sounded like a bird, and all I could hear, I thought, was insects. I sat outdoors patiently for several evenings before a friend suggested listening to a recording of a woodcock.

I located a record of bird songs. To my surprise one of the "insects" turned out to be the woodcock. After I knew what I was listening for, the sound I heard began to sound like the "peent" the books described. But when I heard what I thought were insects, the woodcock was the one that went "bzeep . . . bzeep . . . bzeep" as if it were a tiny electric buzzer.

The best place to listen for a woodcock is near an abandoned field that has begun to grow up into brush. If there are moist woods or wet areas nearby and the whole scene belongs to an abandoned hill farm, the habitat is prime. The best time to listen for the woodcocks' peenting is in the evening just after the sun goes down or early in the morning just as the sun is rising. Woodcocks may, however, go on peenting straight through a bright, moonlit night.

The peent is actually the least interesting part of what the woodcock does. He's only signaling what he's *about* to do. After numerous peents (sometimes as many as 150), the male suddenly spirals upward into a sailing courtship flight designed to win the heart of even the most indifferent female. As he ascends to about 300 feet, his wings twitter and sound like a far-off, high-pitched whistle. For years ornithologists watched and listened and couldn't decide whether the ascending twitter was made by the bird's wings or his voice. Finally, a researcher resolved the matter by removing the three outer primaries (which some people call the "whistling quills") from the wings of a courting male. Without these feathers there was no twitter as the male ascended. As he descended he still sang his flight song of several melodious chirps.

Whether a woodcock's courtship sounds are voice sounds or wing sounds, they all contribute to the drama of his courtship flight. His shrill, twittering ascent seems sudden and breathless. He makes smaller and smaller circles as he climbs, until he seems to stand still high in the darkening sky. Then he glides, zigzagging, back to the ground, chirping as he descends. Once back on the ground, he resumes his peenting in preparation for another flight. The flight itself may take a minute; the peenting may last as long as five minutes. Observers have recorded woodcocks making as many as eighteen flights during one performance.

While the male is performing, the female may be in one of several places. She may not have entered his territory yet, in which case the courtship flight is designed to attract her attention. Or she may have noticed the male already and be waiting patiently on the ground for him to come and mate with her. Sometimes the male and female have already mated, but the male continues his flights for what seems to be the sheer love of flying. Finally, the female may already have laid her eggs and be incubating them nearby, in which case the flight seems to be an entertainment for her—or perhaps an invitation to another female. The female may peent a few times in response to her male's elaborate performance, but she does not participate in his show except to provide him with the occasion for it.

Courtships are the stuff of springtime. If you don't happen to be involved in one yourself and aren't therefore distracted from what's happening all around you, you might enjoy watching the woodcock's unusual method of winning himself a mate. His performance is public (as long as the public watches from a discreet distance), and its exuberant energy will help you feel a part of the celebration of spring.

20

Dandelions

Because my lawn is for me just a place that needs to be mowed, I've never minded dandelions. Their cheerful sunburst faces relieve the monotony of the mowing. The resilience of dandelions that are cut back one day only to reappear the next has always impressed me.

Dandelions are the bold and successful plants they are because they hedge their bets. First of all, they don't limit themselves to restricted habitats. They obviously love lawns, but they will also grow in fields, along roadsides, in vacant lots, and even out of cracks in sidewalks. They grow in both the Northern and Southern Hemispheres. Although they prefer temperate areas, they can be found growing in the Arctic. Their first home was Eurasia, but they have now extended their range around the world.

Part of the reason they have been able to extend their range is their pattern of seed production and dispersal. While many plants produce just one batch of seeds per growing season, dandelions produce new seeds from early spring to late fall. Furthermore, each seed comes equipped with its own private sail to carry it aloft in even the gentlest of breezes. Each spherical seed head you see during the warm months of the year is responsible for another 150 to 200 brand-new dandelion seeds.

Another helpful adaptation is the long perennial taproot that dandelions sink into the soil as they grow. The taproot reaches down deep to absorb moisture and nutrients inaccessible to other plants. This taproot also helps the plant bounce back if its upper parts are injured—by a lawnmower or a determined dandelion picker, for instance.

DANDELION

To raise the flower head into the sunshine the stemless dandelion plant has a flexible hollow stalk that functions even better than a stem. It can grow tall to compete with tall plants, if that's necessary, or stay short to be out of trouble. The stalk bends readily with the wind and weather, saving the flower head from being broken off the plant. When it is time to disperse seeds the stalk grows taller, extending the seed head well into the wind.

Finally, the dandelion's leaves grow in a flat, ground-hugging rosette that keeps the leaves safe and shades out other plants that might try to move in too close. These leaves turn bitter after early spring, so cows and other livestock frequently pass them by. By the time winter snows arrive the dandelion has produced enough leaves to be prepared for its next year's growing season. The leaves wait patiently under the snow all winter and are ready to take advantage of the earliest spring sunshine to start growing again. These early leaves give dandelions an edge over the many biennials and perennials that have to grow new leaves before they can start the season's work.

As if this long list of adaptations weren't enough, the dandelion also has the ability to reproduce whether or not its flowers are pollinated. Its female parts can produce a seed that will grow into a new, genetically identical dandelion without the help of pollen. Now that's the height of efficiency and independence.

I had always thought of the round yellow part of the dandelion as its flower. But actually each little yellow ray is a complete flower in its own right. It's called a floret. You'd need a hand lens to study the construction, but all the parts are there. Each ray is actually five fused petals. You can count the small ridges, which are vestiges of the former petals. If you separate one complete floret from the flower head, you can see its pistil and stamens and its white, bristly sepals. At the base of the floret is the ovary where the mature seed will form.

Before the new flower head is ready to open, green covers called bracts protect it. When the time is right they fold back to expose the florets to the warm sun. They also cover the flower head at night or when it rains. When it comes time for the individual florets to produce their individual seeds, the bracts close for this process, too. They open one last time to expose the fuzzy seed head to the wind.

All in all, dandelions are well-adapted, successful plants. They have managed to travel all over the world and set up communities wherever their seeds have landed. They are so abundant that I can mow them, eat them, pick them, or just play with them idly without feeling guilty about my impact on the species. Although many people consider them weeds, I admire them for the many methods they have developed to ensure their survival.

21

Tent Caterpillars

Spiders aren't the only animals that build homes out of silk. At this time of year it's easy to spot the silken tents of tent caterpillars in the crotches of fruit trees—especially wild cherry and apple. Most people react to tent caterpillars with disgust, for their tents are unsightly, and their eating habits harm trees we value. I certainly don't intend to ask anyone to fall in love with tent caterpillars, but if you look at their life cycle and their adaptations perhaps you can learn to respect their capacity for survival and find intelligent ways to control their invasions.

The tent caterpillar enters the world as an egg laid mid-to-late summer, many months before it appears as a tent-building larva the next spring. The egg layer is a moth. She lays a mass of 200 to 300 eggs on the twig of a tree that the young larvae will feed on the next spring. To protect the eggs from heat, drought, rain, and winter weather, the mother covers them with a varnishlike substance. She dies shortly after she lays her eggs. The next generation of tent caterpillars stays dormant in the protected egg mass through the fall and winter. As a result of this arrangement the species doesn't have to worry about food during the long months when its preferred food—the leaves of fruit trees—is unavailable.

Early the next spring, when the fruit trees begin to bud and grow tender new leaves, the eggs that have waited patiently all winter hatch into small caterpillars. These caterpillars spin silk and build tents to live in during their larval stage. As the tree's leaves grow bigger, so do the caterpillars.

They crawl out of their tents during the day and travel the length of branches and twigs to reach the succulent new leaves of their host tree. To prevent themselves from becoming lost as they crawl all over the tree, each caterpillar spins a strand of silk as it goes and follows it home after feeding.

Very little in the natural world inhibits their progress at this early stage in their development. But along about mid-May a hungry bird returns from the tropics where it has wintered, and it begins feeding on the tent caterpillars. This bird is the cuckoo. In Vermont the most abundant cuckoo is the black-billed cuckoo, but some yellow-billed cuckoos are seen, too. Both thrive on tent caterpillars. An ornithologist studying the eating habits of cuckoos discovered the remains of over 100 tent caterpillars in some of the stomachs he examined.

Because the cuckoos have to feed themselves and eventually their young, the tent caterpillar population is reduced somewhat during the late spring and early summer. But all it takes is one pair that survives into adulthood to produce another egg mass for next year. In mid-to-late June those caterpillars which have avoided the attacks of cuckoos and other predators withdraw into a pupal stage for two and a half weeks' rest. Each individual caterpillar leaves the tent colony and spins itself a tough yellowish cocoon where it pupates. The cocoon may be hidden under bark or in a crevice in a tree. When the adult moth emerges from its cocoon in July, it begins the fourth and final stage of its life cycle. Its last job is to fertilize or lay eggs for the next generation of the species.

Cuckoos kill many of these pests, but if you happen to have a fruit tree or an orchard that you want to protect, maybe you don't want to wait for the cuckoos to arrive or depend on them to eat all the caterpillars you see. One thing you can do when you first see a tent is to cut off the branch the caterpillars are building in. If their tent is in a part of the tree you can't cut away, you can destroy their tent with a kerosene-soaked rag and eliminate the caterpillars a colony at a time. Watch the tent and remove it when most of the caterpillars are "at home."

The next stage of your campaign should be to look for the yellowish cocoons of the pupating insects in late June and early July and destroy the cocoons before the egg-laying adults emerge. Finally, to deal with those which survive both your efforts and the cuckoos' during the summer, spend time during the fall and winter looking for egg masses on the twigs of cherry and apple trees. The egg masses look like shiny brown swellings on the twigs. They're small, but they're easy enough to spot if you're looking for them. When you find one, break off the twig and destroy the whole thing. Better yet, collect the egg masses and count them to estimate the population you would have had to contend with in the spring, and then destroy your collection all at once.

Watchful human beings and hungry cuckoos should be able to keep tent caterpillars in their place. Their reappearance in great numbers each spring, however, is testimony to the species' reproductive and adaptive capacities. Tent caterpillars are a humbling reminder that insects have the edge in the ongoing competition for food and space in this limited world we share.

22

Baby Birds

Every spring the "baby bird crisis" occurs. By May many birds have hatched their first broods and are feeding them in the nest while they grow their feathers and learn to fly. Baby birds have a way of tumbling out of their nests, and children have a way of finding them and bringing them home. What should a family do if faced with this "crisis"?

First, take the baby bird back to the exact spot where it was found. Look carefully for a nest nearby. If you find the nest and it is accessible, put the bird gently back into the nest. Contrary to popular belief, the mother bird will not reject a baby that has been handled by human beings. A deer, which has a keen sense of smell and fears the human scent, will reject a fawn that has been handled, but birds are different. If you find the nest and return the baby, you have done the best you can do.

As a next-best measure, tie a small box onto a branch of a tree or shrub near where the bird was found, and put the baby bird in the box. The bird will thus be off the ground and out of the reach of neighborhood cats and dogs.

The third best thing you can do is simply to leave the bird in the exact spot where it was found. Parent birds are accustomed to having their young fall out of the nest, and they will feed them on the ground. Of course, the baby bird is more vulnerable on the ground than it is in the nest or in a box, but it still stands a better chance of surviving under its own parents' care than under human care. If the baby bird is found near a house, it is better to keep pet dogs and cats indoors than to bring the baby bird indoors in an attempt to protect it.

If the baby is truly abandoned or orphaned—something you can learn only by watching it from a distance for an hour or more—you have a decision to make. You can leave it there to die a natural death—which might in fact be the most humane thing to do. Or you can take it indoors. If you decide to care for it yourself, you are making a substantial commitment. And, even if you live up to your commitment, there is no guarantee that the bird will survive.

BABY BIRDS

Two major problems are involved in trying to parent a baby bird. One is feeding it, and the other is preparing it for life in the wild. Parent birds do it all as a matter of course, but a human parent will have to drop other activities for a period of weeks and perhaps install a screened porch or aviary to do the job right.

Before you can even address yourself to the problem of feeding, however, you have the more immediate problem of the bird's shock and fright to contend with. Perhaps this is the time to send one member of the family for a book on the care of wild animal young, while another rigs up a heating pad or hot water bottle to warm the baby bird. One good book is *Care of the Wild Feathered and Furred: A Guide to Wildlife Handling and Care* (Santa Cruz: Unity Press, 1973) by Mae Hickman and Maxine Guy. Another is Ronald Rood's *The Care and Feeding of Wild Pets* (New York: Pocket Books, 1976). A third book that is specifically about birds is *Bird Ambulance* (New York: Charles Scribner's Sons, 1971) by Arline Thomas.

Now comes the problem of feeding. The warm milk in an eye dropper that seems to be everyone's immediate impulse when it comes to feeding animal young may be appropriate for baby mammals, but it will come as a complete surprise to the baby bird. Its parents were probably feeding it mashed worms, caterpillars, insects, and other delicious odds and ends. Therefore, you'll need to do the same. At first you should supply the baby bird with protein-rich foods. Eventually you're going to have to identify the species and learn something about its food habits in the wild if you want the bird to grow up properly. Whether the bird is a seedeater, an insect eater, or a predator will make a difference.

Parent birds feed their babies about every ten or fifteen minutes from sunrise to sunset. They also feed them exactly what they need to keep their bowels regulated and their bodies growing properly. They also keep the nest clean by removing the babies' excrement, which usually appears shortly after each feeding. In brief, between finding and preparing appropriate food, feeding, and cleaning up after meals you're not going to have much time for anything else for a while if you decide to parent a baby bird.

If you do manage to keep the young bird fed properly and growing, your next problem is providing it with enough space for it to practice flying. You cannot expect a bird to go from your kitchen to the wild with one swoop of its wings. You will need to continue feeding and protecting the bird while it is adjusting to the outdoors. If it had stayed with its parents, it would have had adult birds to follow and imitate, but, with nothing but human beings to encourage it, it will have to make sense out of its environment alone. The young bird that has been raised by humans is at a disadvantage when it comes to competing for food and avoiding the attacks of predators. So even if you do manage to raise a fledgling to adulthood, you have not guaranteed its survival in the wild.

If you think I'm trying to sound discouraging, I am. The adoption of a baby bird will probably result in failure. You might even cause a death that would not have occurred had you left the baby bird where it was. Your intentions might be good; the ethical impulse that motivates your actions might be of the best kind. But you should know that even experienced veterinarians have a low success rate in caring for wild animals.

Perhaps the most important thing a child or adult can learn from an encounter with a baby bird is the difference between wild animals and domestic pets. Whereas puppies and kittens warm to human attention and become very much a part of the family, a wild bird never will. Attempting to make a pet out of a wild animal is a serious disservice to that animal—so serious, in fact, that there are laws against it. Life in the wild does not consist of friendly humans, readily available meals, and a protected environment. Wild animals must remain wild to survive.

Rather than adopt a baby bird, why not "adopt" a whole bird family—from a distance? Chances are there is a bird's nest somewhere near your home. Or you can build birdhouses to attract birds to your yard. Learn to watch the bird family from a distance. If human beings get too close, the parent birds won't come to the nest. So practice sitting quietly, perhaps with a pair of binoculars, far enough away from the nest that the adult birds won't feel threatened.

Watching birds in the wild is a much healthier and more realistic activity than fantasizing that a bird will become your special friend because you raised it. Unfortunately, movies, television, and children's books have created a "Bambi syndrome" in us. The young of most species are precious and adorable, but the desire to fondle and caress and make pets out of wildlings is dangerously romantic. It should not be encouraged. We'd be much wiser if we were content to be observers of wildlife. If we truly care about wild animals, we should be protectors of their wildness, which enables the best of them to survive.

23

Soil

By this time most people have tilled their fields or gardens and planted their crops, vegetables, or flowers. We are now waiting for everything we've planted to grow. Since anyone who farms or gardens has had his or her hands in the soil within the past few weeks, this is an appropriate time to think about where soil comes from, what keeps it alive and healthy, and how it manages to support the variety of life we see around us.

Soil is basically rock, but rock alone is not enough to support life. The rock must be broken down into small particles and mixed with organic matter before plants can anchor themselves in it and find the moisture and nutrients they need to survive. Soil building began with the first winds, rains, and changing temperatures that weathered the barren rocks of the earth's surface. The soils we have now are the product of long years of erosion and weathering, combined with the living and dying of plants and animals.

One unusual plant, the lichen, makes a special contribution to the ongoing process of soil building. Lichens are especially important where glaciers or floods or winds have scoured the surfaces of rocks clean, removing all traces of dust and potential soil particles. Instead of waiting for the forces of erosion to break up the solid rock, lichens attach themselves directly to the rock and manage to make a meager living on exposed surfaces that are otherwise uninhabitable. These rugged little pioneer plants are actually two plants in one. One plant is a fungus that is incapable of manufacturing its own food. Intermeshed with the fungus is an alga that manufactures food for both of them.

Some lichens secrete an acid that eats away at rocks. Others merely expand and contract with hot, cold, wet, and dry weather, pushing and pulling rock particles loose. When lichens die, the organic matter of which they were composed mixes with the rock particles. This mixture may settle into a crack in the rock and provide a potential home for another plant that can't grow on the bare rock itself but can manage with just a little bit of this soil. When mosses and other such small plants find a place to grow, the soil-building process is underway.

Rocks continue to break down with the help of weather, lichens, and the roots of other plants. The plants live and die, providing more and more organic material to mix with the inorganic rock particles. Eventually weeds and grasses will take hold, then shrubs, and finally trees. Ecologists call this orderly change in vegetation *succession.* Finally a *climax* will be reached, and the climax vegetation will live in a carefully balanced equilibrium until something—or someone—comes along to disturb it.

But climax vegetation is a long way from bare rock, and there are other important participants in the preliminary soil-building process. One of the most important jobs is performed by organisms that break down dead plant and animal matter, releasing elements to be used again by living plants and animals. Some of these organisms are microscopic and exist in great numbers in a healthy soil. These are the various kinds of bacteria, fungi, molds, yeasts, and protozoa. Other soil organisms are larger—perhaps you saw some of them while you were working your soil this spring. They include earthworms, millipedes, nematodes, mites, springtails, roundworms, and various insect larvae. These small animals eat plant material and break it down into smaller particles. Their feces fertilize the soil, and their own bodies, when they die, add more organic matter. Finally, there are the larger animals, like moles, which dig tunnels through the soil, loosening and cultivating it as they search for their worm and insect prey.

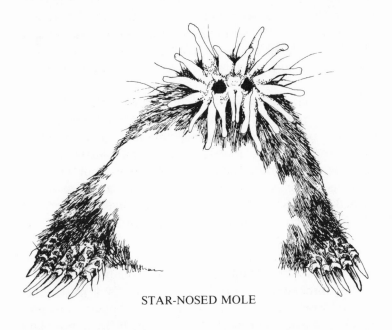

STAR-NOSED MOLE

Once we have soil—rock particles mixed with organic matter from plants and animals, and inhabited by numerous living organisms—how does soil allow our crops to grow? Simple, you say. We plant our seeds, and the sun, rain, and air do the rest. But while the little seedling is struggling up into the sun to manufacture food for the growing plant, its roots are reaching down into the soil looking for the water and minerals it needs to perform its life processes.

A plant needs not just carbon, hydrogen, and oxygen—which it can get from air and water—but also phosphorus, potassium, nitrogen, sulfur, calcium, iron, and magnesium, plus small quantities of copper, zinc, boron, manganese, and molybdenum. These minerals enter land plants through their roots, and they must be in a water solution to be available to the plant.

The soil first of all provides a place for the plant to grow its roots. These roots anchor the plant while it is performing all the complex processes necessary to life and growth. In return, the plant's roots anchor the soil, slowing down the determined forces that would carry the soil off to the sea.

In addition to giving plants a place to sink their roots, the soil holds water and allows it to circulate and dissolve the mineral salts the plant needs to survive. The mineral salts come from the parent rock particles. They dissolve in water or a weak acid formed by water and carbon dioxide and become individual electrically charged units called ions. It is these ions that the plant absorbs through its roots.

In addition to providing anchorage, minerals, and water to dissolve the minerals, soil also holds pockets of air. Specialized bacteria work on the nitrogen in this air to produce the nitrate that a plant needs to make proteins. The air also provides oxygen for the respiration of the organisms that live and work in the soil.

The next time you pick up a handful of soil, think about what went into making it and the ongoing processes that maintain it. As long as our soil is alive and well, our plants will thrive, and we who live on plants and plant-eating animals will survive. If our soil dies or disappears, however, we'll have to wait a long time for the natural forces of erosion and the pioneer work of lichens to set the long and complex process of soil building in motion again.

24

Red Efts

One of the first animals I encountered when I began paying attention to the natural world was a red eft. I was taking a late spring walk when I spotted a small, brightly colored creature on the forest floor. A delicate little thing, brilliant red-orange, it stood absolutely still on the moist leaf litter. I spent a long time trying to figure out what it was. My only thought was that it might be an escaped chameleon someone had bought at a circus or pet shop.

RED EFT

At the time, I wasn't clear on the differences between lizards and salamanders, let alone where newts, efts, and chameleons might fit in. Finding that red eft made me begin to make some important distinctions.

First of all, to distinguish between chameleons and red efts it's necessary to distinguish between reptiles and amphibians. Reptiles have protective scales or plates for skin, and their toes (if they have any) have claws. Their young hatch from eggs and are miniatures of their parents. Class Reptilia includes crocodiles, alligators, turtles, snakes, and lizards. Chameleons are reptiles, belonging to the lizard family.

Amphibians, in contrast, have moist skin filled with mucus-secreting glands, and they have no claws on their toes. Their young pass through a larval stage that's usually aquatic, and then they metamorphose into terrestrial—or sometimes aquatic—adults. Class Amphibia includes frogs and toads, salamanders and newts, and an obscure tropical group called caecilians.

Where do red efts fit in? They are phase two of the three-phase life cycle of an amphibian called the red-spotted newt. Actually newts and efts aren't different animals at all. The only reason we have different words for them is somebody's carelessness a long time ago. The original English word for them was the Anglo-Saxon *efete,* meaning lizardlike. In Middle English the word became *evete* or *ewete.* Because in English we use the indefinite article *an* with a noun beginning with a vowel, when people talked about one of these creatures they said *an ewete.*

Somewhere along the line, when someone was writing about this creature, he wrote *a newete,* and the error evolved into the separate and seemingly unrelated word *newt.* So now we have the two modern English words *newt* and *eft* to confuse us when we're actually talking about the same animal.

Newt usually refers to the aquatic stages of this creature's life—its babyhood and adulthood. *Eft* is reserved for the one- to three-year period when it takes to the land to roam the moist woods. During the terrestrial period its color changes from the green-brown of its early aquatic phase to the orange-red that caught my eye against the leaf litter. When it returns to the water as an adult, it turns green-brown again.

The red eft, being an amphibian, is sensitive to temperature and moisture. In winter it hibernates under a rotting log. During warmer months it is active, but it spends much of its time hiding in moist places. The best time to see one is just after a rain, when efts take advantage of the moisture to move around. Their brilliant color is no disadvantage when they choose to reveal themselves, for any animal that tries to eat a red eft has to deal with the poisonous secretions the eft emits when alarmed. Its color is therefore a bright flag to warn would-be predators to keep their distance.

Technically, newts (and therefore efts) are salamanders of the family Salamandridae, but their skin, especially in the eft stage, is not quite as slippery as the skin of other salamanders. Also, they have an aquatic adulthood following the terrestrial eft stage, whereas most salamanders that are called salamanders remain terrestrial.

It's confusing to have so many different words for closely related animals, but it wasn't until relatively recently that zoologists began to make distinctions and classifications that now give similar Latin names to animals that belong together in similar evolutionary groups. Because the English words we use to refer to the animals we see around us have a history more ancient than modern zoology, we will have to live with the confusing common names animals go by. I can't say that I blame the Anglo-Saxons for using a word that meant lizardlike for the first newts and efts they saw. Left to my own vocabulary, I would have confused the matter totally by calling the first red eft I saw a chameleon.

25

Mosquitoes

Mosquitoes can be counted on to ruin summer parties, picnic suppers, cookouts, and other evening recreations. Actually, I don't mind them so much when I'm outdoors because I don't hear them. But when I'm lying in bed at night just about ready to doze off, or early in the morning before I'm really ready to get out of bed, the high-pitched whine of a hungry mosquito is enough to destroy my basically positive attitude toward living things.

It doesn't help any to know that the whining offender is a female in search of the meal of blood she needs to produce her eggs. With the help of my blood she will add insult to injury by going off to lay 100 to 400 eggs, many of which will grow up into another generation of blood-hungry females.

The female mosquito has mouthparts well-adapted for piercing skin and sucking blood. What looks like a long pointed nose is actually her lower lip, which serves as a carrying case for her specialized mouthparts. Resting inside the lower lip are two mandibles and two maxillae, which, instead of serving as lower and upper jaws for chewing, serve as sharp needles for piercing. A special salivary channel and a thin, pointed upper lip complete the mosquito's tools.

After the female mosquito lands on a likely blood donor, she positions her lower lip to guide her "needles" into the spot she has selected. First, the mandibles and maxillae make a hole, then the salivary channel and upper lip begin their work. The mosquito injects some saliva to keep the blood from clotting during the operation, and the upper lip sucks the blood straight into her swelling gut.

Although the males do not bite, suck blood, or make irritating sounds, they are not blameless in this matter. They respond to the female's high-pitched flight song—the same one that drives me crazy—with a desire to mate. The male flies to the whining female, mates with her, and soon thereafter dies. He has done his part in producing the next generation of mosquitoes.

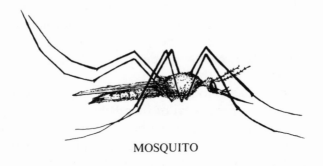

MOSQUITO

Mosquitoes aren't much fun to have around, but, unfortunately, we are stuck with them—about 2,000 different species of them worldwide. We can be thankful, at least, that the common house mosquito is not a carrier of diseases. If we lived in the tropics, we'd have to sleep with mosquito nets and worry about more than petty irritations. Some tropical mosquitoes carry organisms that cause malaria, yellow fever, encephalitis, and elephantiasis. Attempts to control these disease-carrying insects with pesticides have merely produced pesticide-resistant insects. Researchers are still working on ways to outsmart and control mosquitoes.

Meanwhile, the best way to deal with the mosquitoes in your life is to understand their mating habits and life cycle and to combat them at all stages. With adults, the best control is to swat them. A dead male could mean an unmated female, and an unmated female—or a dead one—means as many as 400 unlaid eggs.

If you don't kill the parents, the first stage in the next generation's life cycle is the egg. Mosquitoes lay their eggs in water, and both larvae and pupae are aquatic. One way to keep mosquito eggs and young away from your house is to eliminate standing water. These pests need only a little water—sometimes as little as the rain that collects in a mud puddle or an old can. If you drain or cover the water, you deprive breeding mosquitoes of a necessity.

If the water around your house is permanent or necessary to you or your animals, keep watch for the tightly packed masses of eggs. These floating egg rafts can't survive out of water. Therefore all you have to do is remove them to dry land. If you miss the eggs and they hatch, you'll have to combat the active larvae and pupae. You can introduce aquatic predators to the water. Minnows and sunfish love young mosquitoes. Dragonfly and damselfly nymphs, water bugs, and water boatmen are other helpful predators.

If the mosquitoes manage to survive your eradication programs and reach adulthood, you might cope with them by adopting a scientific interest in their behavior. The male will apparently respond to sounds at frequencies close to his lady love's flight song. Drive him crazy with a tuning fork. The female is apparently attracted to carbon dioxide. Breathe on her, and lure her close enough to have a good look at her, before you swat her.

If all else fails and you find that yet another mosquito has just bitten you, don't waste energy on what it's too late to do anything about. Consider surrounding yourself with spiders, bats, dragonflies, and insect-eating birds. In the ensuing competition, if the predators' appetites win out over the mosquitoes' reproductive capacity, you will be saved. Thanks to the hungry predators, your blood and your sanity will be preserved.

26

Dragonflies

On a recent canoe trip the group I was with stopped for lunch near a concrete dam. As I leaned back against one end of the dam, I noticed what looked like an ugly brown water bug locked in combat with a winged insect of some kind. When I looked more closely, however, I discovered that the two insects were actually one. A dragonfly was emerging from the skin that had encased it while it was growing to adulthood.

I watched the dragonfly extricate itself. It did not seem especially like a dragon as it twitched and strained to rid itself of the old shell. Its wings were crumpled as if they had been jammed too tightly into a space too small. They expanded gradually, but, even after the adult dragonfly was completely free of the shell, its wings still looked bedraggled and useless.

The dragonfly seemed exhausted by its struggle, but it crawled weakly along the dam, its wings only very slowly filling out toward their full size. By the time I had to leave, it still looked more like a whipped and wounded old warrior than a brand new dragonfly about to embark on its adult career.

Some insects, such as moths and butterflies, have what's called a complete metamorphosis. They go through four distinct stages as they grow into adults. Born as eggs, they hatch into larvae, then have a resting period during which they are called pupae, and finally emerge as completely formed adults.

The dragonfly goes through only three stages, so its

metamorphosis is called incomplete. From the egg it hatches into what's called a nymph. The nymph grows and molts its outgrown skin several times. Finally, when the adult dragonfly is ready to emerge, the nymph's skin splits one last time, and the adult insect struggles free. The dragonfly misses the resting period between youth and adulthood. It has done all its changing while it was growing inside the nymph's protective shell.

The dragonfly's life cycle somewhat resembles an amphibian's. As an adult the dragonfly lives in the air with all the necessary equipment for an aerial existence, but, like an amphibian, it must return to water to lay its eggs. The young nymphs that hatch from the eggs are suited only for an aquatic existence. The nymph doesn't look any more like an adult dragonfly than a tadpole looks like a frog. But instead of growing adult equipment a bit at a time as the tadpole does, the nymph grows into a bigger and bigger nymph with the adult dragonfly evolving inside the nymph's skin. The final molt brings the aquatic nymph out of the water, where its split skin reveals the fully formed adult.

The dragonfly nymph has little in common with the adult insect other than its voracious appetite for other insects. It is an ugly brown water creature that lurks in the dark places of a pond, lake, or slow-moving stream. When an unsuspecting insect or even a small fish or tadpole swims too close, the dragonfly nymph extends its long, jointed lower jaw, which is equipped with grappling hooks, and snatches its prey.

The adult dragonfly doesn't wait in ambush. It pursues its prey aggressively. A speedy and competent flier, it catches its prey mid-flight—not with a fancy jaw like the nymph's but with its legs. The legs have stiff bristles, and the dragonfly holds them together like a basket, scooping up insects as it flies.

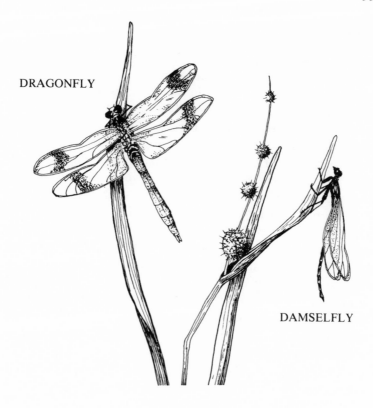

DRAGONFLY

DAMSELFLY

The dragonfly nymph is capable of fast enough motion when it's in a hurry, but its means of locomotion is totally unrelated to the adult's ability to fly. Its underwater movement is closely related to its underwater breathing. The nymph has gills located at the end of its alimentary canal. It takes in water by expanding its abdomen, the water washes over the gills, the gills absorb what oxygen the nymph needs, and then the abdomen contracts and expels the water. The nymph can expel this water with enough force to move forward at a considerable speed. It uses this water propulsion to dart away from danger and sometimes to pursue prey.

The dragonfly is well adapted to survive as an aquatic nymph during the early stage of its life, and is equally well adapted to an adulthood in the air. Its long history is testimony to the success of its adaptations. Its ancestors date back to the Carboniferous period, 320 million years ago. Scientists have found fossils of large dragonflylike insects with wingspans of up to thirty inches. Other flying insects of the Carboniferous period are now extinct, but the dragonfly—although much smaller these days—still persists.

One place to look for dragonflies is near still or slow-moving water. If you look into the water you might spot the aquatic nymph, but its brown color serves as excellent camouflage. You can catch it with a net if you want a close look. If it's a sunny day, you're more likely to see the handsome adult flying above the water or around the neighboring meadows and roads, scooping up mosquitoes and other small insects as it goes.

The only other insect you might confuse with a dragonfly is the damselfly, which is a close relative. The damselfly is smaller and tends to hover around the grasses at the edge of a pond or stream rather than fly boldly and aggressively through the air. At rest the damselfly holds its wings together above its back. The dragonfly rests with its wings outstretched.

Once you've become a keen enough observer to tell damselflies from dragonflies, you might want to go a step further and distinguish some of the different species within each group. If you're as lucky as I was the day I went canoeing, you might even happen upon a dragonfly at the moment of transition and witness the amazing change from ugly brown water nymph to magnificent aerial adult.

Summer

27

Fireflies

Firefly, lightning bug, and glowworm are all common names for the same insect, and all are misleading. First, the insect that goes by these names is not a "fly" or a "bug" or a "worm." It is a beetle. A beetle is characterized by stiff front wings that fold back over the membranous hind wings to protect them when they're not being used for flying. The adult females in some species of fireflies are flightless, and these flightless females, which emit light signals from the ground, are what some people call glowworms. Some people also call firefly larvae glowworms.

"Fire," "lightning," and "glow" are also misleading. They all imply heat, while the firefly's light is a cold light. The chemical process that produces it gives off almost no heat. Even though their common names are misleading, the insects I'm talking about are familiar to anyone who has stood outdoors on a warm June night. Their life cycle and habits demonstrate some of the insect world's most amazing achievements.

The obvious place to begin in talking about fireflies is with the light they make. They can make this light at will, and each species has its own flash code. In most instances it's the male that flies around emitting tentative light signals, while the female stays near the ground responding to the male's messages with her own coded responses. A pair that has made contact may exchange from five to ten signals before they mate.

There is one notable exception to this typical pattern of courtship and mating. The predatory females of one genus (*Photuris*) mimic the response signals of other females and lure unsuspecting males to their death. One of these females can emit the mating responses of two or three other fireflies in order to eat the males that fall for her performance. She can also emit the appropriate code to invite a male of her own species to come mate with her. The nerve impulses that tell her luminescent organs whether she wants to mate or eat must be complex indeed.

The desire to mate (or eat) does not completely explain the firefly's luminescence, however. The eggs and larvae of some fireflies are luminescent, too, and they certainly are not sending out mating signals. The leading authorities on fireflies theorize that early in the earth's history the atmosphere was devoid of free oxygen. The organisms that lived during those early days were adapted to life without oxygen. When free oxygen began to be a component of the atmosphere, it may have been toxic to some of these early organisms. Some of them therefore developed bioluminescence, an oxygen-consuming process, as a way of getting rid of undesired oxygen by burning it inside their bodies.

Later in evolutionary history when large quantities of atmospheric oxygen became an established fact, organisms learned to use it and became dependent upon it for their life processes. Some organisms, however, retained the old oxygen-burning, light-emitting process because they had found practical uses for the phenomenon. Fireflies retained it as a unique and effective method of attracting mates.

The chemical process that creates the firefly's light has fascinated scientists for many years. Researchers have succeeded in analyzing and isolating all the substances involved, but they have not yet developed a lighting system that burns as efficiently as the firefly's mating beacon. Bioluminescence is called "cold light" because less than one percent of the energy released in producing the light is released in the form of heat. Fluorescent lights, on the other hand, emit 78 percent heat and 22 percent light, and incandescent light bulbs give 90 percent heat with only 10 percent light.

The chemical reaction that creates the firefly's light takes place in specialized cells located in the sixth and seventh segments of the abdomen. These cells, called photocytes, contain a fatty substance that emits light when oxidized. It's called luciferin. The fatty tissue is permeated with little air tubes that deliver the oxygen and a nerve network that conveys the signal to start the chemical reaction that results in light. Basically, four substances interact in the presence of oxygen to create the light: the organic compound luciferin, an enzyme called luciferase, an energy-rich compound called adenosine triphosphate (ATP), and magnesium.

Although the firefly's light is what scientists have paid most attention to, the period during which the firefly uses this light for mating is the shortest period of its life. The firefly is born as one of a hundred or so eggs laid in the soil or leaf litter during the summer. It hatches after three or four weeks and spends its first summer as an active predatory larva. It eats snails, slugs, and earthworms. When cold weather comes it digs down into the soil and becomes inactive for the cold months. The next spring it emerges for another season of eating and growing. It isn't until the next spring that the two-year-old larva will pupate for ten days and emerge as a full-grown adult prepared to mate—and shortly thereafter to die.

If you're interested in observing a firefly up close, it's not difficult to catch one. You can grab a male as he flies by, or you can scoop a female from the grass. If you're more interested in their communication system than in the details of their physical appearance, you can focus on a pair of the same species and study the duration of their flashes, the number of flashes in each flash pattern, the intervals between flashes and flash patterns, and the length of time the female waits before she flashes back in response to the male. If you're not interested in these scientific approaches, you can just sit outdoors on a summer evening and enjoy the free light show provided by your neighborhood fireflies.

28

Buttercups

Yellow must be one of nature's favorite colors. It is bestowed liberally on common wildflowers. If you look closely, however, you will notice that each yellow is different. With dandelions it's a sunburst yellow for the entire flower head. With daisies it's a greenish yellow for the small flowers clustered in the center. With black-eyed Susans it's a tawny yellow for the rays. Buttercups have their own yellow that gives them part of their name. It's a rich buttery yellow that looks like a smooth coat of enamel covering the inside of the petals. You can turn the flower upside down to see what the same color looks like without the gloss.

Buttercups are very different from dandelions, daisies, or black-eyed Susans. Each buttercup is a single flower with each of its flower parts plainly visible. The other flowers have flower heads composed of numerous separate flowers, each with its own tiny flower parts, which are too small to see without a hand lens. They are called composites and represent a relatively modern development in the evolution of flowers. Buttercups, on the other hand, are quite primitive. In fact, many botanists believe that a primitive buttercup was the ancestor of all our modern flowering plants.

It's hard to imagine the familiar buttercup playing such an important role in evolutionary history. Whatever its historical role, the buttercup is a good flower to learn about because it is familiar, abundant, and fairly simple in construction. It is a complete flower, which means that it has all four flower parts—petals, sepals, stamens (male), and pistils (female). You can see each of these parts without much difficulty. The five yellow petals attract our attention in the first place. Under the petals are five greenish-yellow sepals. Within the cup formed by the petals are the stamens, or male parts, which produce pollen, and the pistils, or female parts, which need to be pollinated.

COMMON BUTTERCUP

The stamens are the little yellow hairs standing inside the cup. With a hand lens you can see that the hairs are actually capsules at the tops of short stalks. These capsules contain the pollen to fertilize a new generation of buttercup seeds. If you brush all the stamens back, you will see a tight green growth at the center of the flower. It looks like the tip of the stem protruding right into the cup. It consists of several individual ovaries, each of which, if fertilized, will produce a separate seed. If you can find a buttercup that's gone by, you will see an enlarged version of the female parts. Once the bright yellow petals have done their job of attracting insect pollinators and the stamens have released their pollen, all the flower parts except the fertilized female parts fall away. The green cluster left at the tip of each buttercup stem will mature into seeds, which will disperse to become new buttercups.

With male and female parts so close together in the same flower, you'd think it would be almost automatic that each flower would pollinate itself, but that is not the case. The male parts usually mature and produce their pollen before the females parts of the same flower are ready to be pollinated. Insects crawling in and out of the buttercups in search of nectar carry pollen from the mature males to females that are ready to receive it, so most buttercups are cross-pollinated rather than self-pollinated. Cross-pollination is better for the development of the species.

On each buttercup plant you can find buttercup flowers at all stages of their life cycle: buds, young flowers, older flowers, and flowers turned to seed heads. If you happen to notice an insect in one of the open flowers, you might want to know where it finds the nectar it's after. If you pull out one of the buttercup petals, you will see a small scale attached to the base of the petal where it was connected to the flower. That scale protects the nectary. A hungry insect has to work its body through a lot of pollen to get at the nectar that's hidden at the base of each petal.

Buttercups are so common that many people consider them weeds. They grow prolifically along roadsides and in moist fields. Because cows and other livestock don't like their acrid taste, you will find lots of buttercups in pastures. Although it's easy to ignore a flower that is everywhere, I think buttercups are worth knowing about. Their direct relationship to the ancestral buttercup that may have given us all our modern flowers should give them special status among their more modern cousins.

29

Bees, Wasps, and Hornets

If you've just been stung, you probably don't care whether it was a bee, a wasp, or a hornet. But if you take the time to learn some of the differences among these insects, maybe you can avoid being stung in the future.

First of all, a bee is never a wasp, and a wasp is not always a hornet, but all hornets are always wasps. That is not a riddle but a way of introducing the relationships among three names used almost interchangeably in casual conversation. Bees, wasps, and hornets—and ants too—all belong to the same order of insects, the Hymenoptera, or "membrane-winged." Within this order honeybees and bumblebees belong to one family, and wasps belong to several different families. Hornets belong to the wasp family called Vespidae and are characterized by their short tempers and painful stings.

One basic difference between bees and wasps is that bees feed their young plant food (pollen, nectar, and honey) while wasps feed their young animal food (caterpillars, other insect larvae, and in many instances spiders). Bees and wasps look different, too. Bees' bodies are rounder and hairier than wasps' bodies.

Bees and wasps are alike in that the adults all feed on pollen, nectar, sweet fruit juices, and other plant foods. Also, the ovipositors of the infertile females are adapted as stingers. Some species of wasps use these stingers to paralyze prey. Bees and other wasps use them strictly as weapons of defense. It's the short-tempered hornets that are most likely to use their stingers on human beings.

The stingers common to all these insects encourage us to blur distinctions, ignore behavioral differences, and not even consider ecological roles. We tend to think of the bees and wasps we encounter as direct threats to our well-being. Actually, most bees and wasps are not even interested in us. They don't need our blood as food, and they can't paralyze us to feed to their young, so they stand to gain nothing from stinging us.

Why do they sting us, then? Many bees and wasps are social insects, and one of the duties of a social insect is to defend its colony. If you are stung, most likely the bee or wasp that stung you perceived you as a threat to its colony.

Yellow jackets, which are sometimes called hornets, and white-faced hornets are the most aggressive of the social wasps. Because they are so intent upon defending their colonies, I keep my distance from them. Yellow jackets usually build underground, but I've found their gray paper nests in old buildings, too. White-faced hornets spend an entire season creating their football-size nest, only to be wiped out wholesale by fall frosts. The next spring the fertile queens, which are the only members of the colony to survive the winter, will start new colonies all over again. The members of each new colony will spend their short, busy lives building and defending a new nest and feeding another generation of young.

Another species of social wasps, called polistes wasps, are much less aggressive than their hornet cousins. They build a small gray nest that looks like an open honeycomb hanging from a porch ceiling or the eaves of a house. They don't cause human beings much trouble, but, because they build their nests near where we live, they are frequently sprayed or destroyed for fear of their sting. Their open, honeycomb nests show the individual brood chambers where the queen lays her eggs. Because polistes wasps are not aggressive, you can watch their activities closely. What you see happening will give you a good idea of what goes on inside the covered or buried nests of other social wasps.

In addition to these social wasps, there are also many species of solitary wasps. Some live in hollow twigs, and some make nests of mud or clay. These solitary wasps don't bother human beings at all because they don't act in groups to maintain and protect a colony. The females work alone to build a nest, provide each cell with a paralyzed insect or spider, and lay their eggs. The solitary female would probably fly away from you if you approach her. She would only sting you as a last resort.

Honeybees and bumblebees are both social, but they are not aggressive. Honeybees nest in man-made hives or in hollow trees, while bumblebees nest underground. The entire colony of honeybees stays alive through the winter, sharing body heat and living on stored honey. Bumblebees, on the other hand, are killed by the cold weather. Only the mated queens survive to start new colonies in the spring. They hibernate in an old log, in the bark of a tree, or sometimes inside a building.

Although bees and wasps are probably best known for their stings (the honeybee's honey running a close second), they are actually great helpers to human beings. Bees are the best pollinators of all the pollinating insects. Many of our agricultural crops depend on them. Wasps are helpful, too, especially as insect and spider controls. Because they feed their numerous young on insects and spiders, they are an important part of nature's checks and balances. Next time you hear the familiar buzz that alerts you to a bee or wasp, take a close look at the insect before you swat or run. Learn to recognize yellow jackets and white-faced hornets so you can avoid them, and let the others go about their business.

30

Ants

Ants are close relatives of bees and wasps. During the summer, I see them—hundreds of them—everywhere I look. I watch columns of small black ants parading single file along the windowsills of my kitchen. I walk out my front door and I see anthills around the flat stones of my path. I visit my garden and see ants crawling on the flowers. I walk down my dirt road and see anthills all along both sides. Even when I go into town, I see anthills erupting from the cracks of sidewalks.

Ants are abundant because they are well-adapted and successful insects. The twentieth century does not seem to be bothering them at all. Unlike many other abundant and successful animals, however, it's not the well-adapted individual that spells their success. It's their well-adapted communities. One ant left to its own devices would lose all its motivation for survival. Individual behavior is related to life in the community, and without the community an individual ant wouldn't know what to do.

Workers, who are infertile females, constitute the most numerous caste in ant society. The queen, a caste of one, lays all the eggs for the colony, while the winged males exist only to accompany an unmated queen on her wedding flight. They die shortly after the queen's eggs have been fertilized.

The worker's life consists of repeated routines motivated by the needs of the community. The youngest workers are nurses. They care for the eggs, larvae, and pupae of the ant colony, spending most of their waking hours transporting eggs and immature young from one part of the nest to another. They feed the larvae and lick them, receiving a sweet substance in return. They also protect the inactive pupae. Because nurses are homebound, they depend on older food-gathering workers for the food they and their charges need to survive. Some ant species also have another group of workers, which are soldiers. Their job is to protect the colony from attack and destruction.

The behavior of each individual worker interlocks with the behavior of all other members of the colony. Whenever two ants encounter one another, no matter what their tasks, they pause to feel each other with their antennae and exchange a drop of special food. Stored in a compartment called a crop, which is separate from the digestive system, this special food is a mixture of everything the ant has been eating and exchanging with the other ants. The larvae contribute one of the most important ingredients. Apparently, the sweet larval emissions, licked by the nurses and passed throughout the colony by means of the constant food exchanging, motivate the food gatherers to keep gathering food, the nurses to keep nursing, and the queen to keep laying eggs—or perhaps to stop for a while.

In addition to the food exchanges, which keep the motivating chemicals moving throughout the colony, the individual ant also needs behavior models. The examples provided by other ants help each ant perform its tasks. Some older ants have been doing their jobs for so long that they have become very good at them. These "work starters" provide the example for less experienced ants to follow, and soon the entire colony is busy at their interlocking tasks.

Most of what an ant needs to know is inborn. The first five segments of its sensitive antennae help it interpret its surroundings and respond appropriately. In the early 1900s a scientist named Adele Fielde performed some fascinating experiments and determined that each of the first five segments of an ant's antennae controls a different aspect of its social behavior. The end segment, for instance, detects the odor of the ant's nest to keep it from entering a strange colony. The next segment can detect the odor that tells whether another ant is descended from the same queen. The third segment detects the odor the ant itself left as it walked along, giving it a scent trail to follow home. The fourth and fifth segments respond to the young and dictate proper care. If something happens to any or all of these five segments, the ant loses its ability to function within the colony, and its days are numbered.

Different species of ants have evolved different ways of living, but all ants live socially. Some ant societies are strangely similar to human societies. The army ants of Africa and South America might be described as hunter-nomads. They roam and hunt for a while, then they settle and raise young for a while. The leaf-cutting ants of South America (and as far north as Louisiana and Texas) are farmers. They cut bits of leaves and bring them home, where they become beds for cultivating a special fungus that the ants eat. Some of the commonest ants in New England are what might be called dairying ants. They tend herds of aphids that suck plant juices. The ants, in turn, "milk" the aphids by stroking them with their antennae until the aphids offer drops of a sweet substance called honeydew. New England also has slave-keeping ants. Slave-keepers will attack the nest of another species and rob it of its young. The slave-keepers will then raise the young to keep house for them.

Ants of the same colony never squabble or fight, but ants from different species, or even just different colonies, will fight fiercely over slaves, food, or territorial rights. All in all, an ant's life is not a bad life—if you can accept the premise that the colony is more important than the individual. Ants have no trouble with this premise because it is impossible for an individual to survive without signals from the rest of the group.

The ants' communal approach to survival gives them the double advantage of numbers and division of labor. They have used these advantages to compete successfully for a long time. If the populations sustained by ants in my neighborhood are any indication of their larger welfare, I think it's safe to say that ants are doing okay.

31

Raspberries

Mid-summer has its shortcomings, with hot days, dusty roads, weedy gardens, and buzzing insects, but it also has its glories. One of the nicest things about July is raspberries. Red raspberries come first, and I race birds and other wildlife to get the delicious red fruits. Then, a week or so after red raspberries, black raspberries start ripening.

Red and black raspberries are closely related and have much in common, but they are also different in several ways. Showing their kinship, both plants are perennial and can produce berries for many years. Both also have a biennial growth pattern. New canes grow one year and produce berries the next. After they've produced their berries, the two-year-old canes die.

As for the differences—besides the color, texture, and taste of their fruits—red raspberry canes are thinner and shorter, and the prickers aren't as sharp. They spread by sending up suckers from their roots. Black raspberries spread from the other end. Their longer, heavier canes arc downward until they touch the ground and root to form new plants.

Two other common berries are closely related to red and black raspberries. One is the purple flowering raspberry. Its flower is much showier than the flowers of the other raspberries, but the fruits taste dry and bland by contrast. I eat them, too, but they are not in the same league with their juicier cousins. The blackberry, which is still a hard green cluster when the red and black raspberries ripen, is another close relative. Blackberries aren't quite as sweet as raspberries, and when you pick one the entire berry including the central core comes away. There's something about the hollow center of the other raspberries that contributes to their special taste and texture.

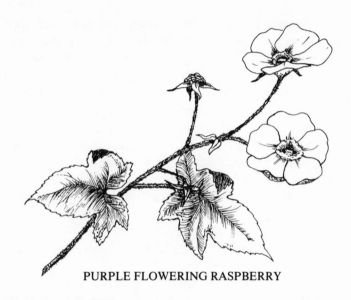

PURPLE FLOWERING RASPBERRY

Although everyone thinks of raspberries and blackberries as berries, actually they are not true berries. The classification of fruits is enough to confuse even a dedicated botanist. A true berry, for instance, has seeds in the center, a fleshy pulp around the seeds, and a skin around the pulp. Strangely enough, oranges and lemons are true berries, and so are grapes and tomatoes.

Raspberries consist of numerous small spheres clinging together around a central receptacle. If you chew a raspberry thoughtfully, or disassemble one to study its parts, you will notice that each little sphere has its own skin, its own fleshy pulp, and its own seed. A one-seeded fruit with the seed or stone at the center of a fleshy pulp is called a drupe. Cherries, peaches, and plums are drupes. Technically, raspberries and blackberries are aggregates of drupelets rather than true berries.

It's less important to me, however, what kind of fruit raspberries are than how they taste. Red raspberries fresh from the bush, soft and still warm from the sun, are my favorite fruit. Even the tropics don't produce a competitor. Most fruits contain compounds called esters that contribute sweet and distinctive tastes, and raspberries have an unusual number of them. While cherries have three, apricots four, and strawberries five, raspberries have a delicious nine that make them the special taste treat they are.

I'm not the only one who likes raspberries. My book on wildlife food habits tells me that ninety-seven different species of birds and animals eat raspberries and blackberries. I can't claim to have seen all ninety-seven of them eating my raspberries, but I know the fruits disappear all too fast once they've ripened. In addition to eating the ripe fruits, some animals also eat the young canes and leaves. Many small birds and mammals also use the pricker bushes for cover. Brer Rabbit and Peter Cottontail have made the briar patch famous for more than just berries.

Raspberries are a symbol of summer for me. With raspberry bushes growing around the edges of my yard, I find frequent excuses to take breaks from weeding my garden or working indoors. A handful of fresh raspberries helps me keep the heat, dust, weeds, and insects of these long summer days in proper perspective.

32

Galls

Have you ever noticed a hard green ball—or several of them—growing partway up a goldenrod stem? That growth is a gall. Not all galls are as round and obvious as this familiar goldenrod gall, but they all have something in common. They are abnormal growths of plant tissue caused by an organism other than the plant itself. Most galls you see are caused by insects, but some are also caused by mites, nematodes, bacteria, fungi, and viruses.

The basic process involved in gall formation has long fascinated scientists and medical researchers because of the possible relationship between plant galls and human tumors. Exactly what happens to make a gall develop is still a subject of debate and research, but it involves a substance or substances that gall makers introduce into the host plant. The gall maker's secretion causes the cells of the host plant to enlarge or multiply or do both. The result is an abnormal growth on whichever part of the plant the gall maker has chosen: stem, leaf, root, bud, flower, or twig.

Each gall maker chooses a specific plant and a particular part of that specific plant. The goldenrod ball gall is caused by a small fly that lays its egg in the stem of the common goldenrod. Either the female, when she deposits her egg in the stem, or the larva, when it first hatches from the egg—or perhaps both of them—secretes a substance that irritates the goldenrod. The plant then grows the solid spherical structure that provides both food and shelter for the growing larva.

The goldenrod ball gall is self-limiting; it will grow only as long as the larva within it continues to cause it to grow. Some other types of galls are tumorous. They continue to grow amorphously long after the organism that caused the gall to start has left. All of the self-limiting galls have a characteristic shape, size, and structure that is related to the organism that causes them. Because gall makers are host-specific, and because the self-limiting galls have a characteristic appearance, gall identification can aid in both plant and insect identification.

From the insect's point of view, the advantages of a gall are numerous. The little larva that hatches inside the goldenrod ball gall has both food and protection right where it is. It eats the extra plant tissue inside the gall and grows until it's ready to pupate. Just before it pupates it eats its way almost out of the gall, leaving just a very thin wall between itself and the outside world. When the adult fly emerges from the pupa, all it has to do is break through the last paper-thin wall.

But life is not perfect for insect gall makers. Galls are visible, and birds and rodents have learned to look at galls as likely places to find tasty bits of food. Other insects parasitize gall makers. They let the gall maker create the gall, and then they move in to feed on the gall maker. Some galls become complex social environments, with the excess plant tissue providing housing and food not just for the original gall maker, but for another insect that parasitizes the gall maker, and maybe even for another that parasitizes the parasite. Other insects may move in just for the free plant food. And still others may lay eggs or winter in the spacious interior of a used gall.

One of the most interesting things about galls is that they can grow on one or perhaps several parts of the plant without seriously damaging it. Although a few types of galls are crippling or even deadly to the host plant, most self-limiting galls don't do much harm. It wouldn't be correct to call the relationship between the insect and the plant symbiotic because the plant receives nothing in return for the food and shelter it provides for the insect. But the relationship does seem to be basically nondestructive.

Although gall makers are host-specific, that does not mean that each plant attracts only one type of gall maker. The goldenrod plays host to at least three that I've seen. I notice the work of the ball gall maker most readily. A small moth causes a more elliptical enlargement on goldenrod stems. A third gall maker, a midge, causes a tightly bunched cluster of extra leaves to form at the top of the goldenrod plant. Oak trees are much more popular than goldenrods, with nearly 800 gall makers finding them their preferred host plant. I'm most familiar with "oak apples," which look like puffballs growing on oak leaves.

Galls fascinate me because they represent such ingenious adaptations on the part of the gall makers and such curious and sometimes beautiful responses on the part of the host plants. The question I find myself asking is how did the first gall maker get its start? Because there are about 2,000 different types of galls in the United States alone, and therefore at least 2,000 successful gall makers, it is obvious that, however gall making began, it works. Galls are just one visible example of the unusual relationships organisms have discovered in their constant struggle for survival.

33

Queen Anne's Lace

Queen Anne's lace is one of our commonest and most abundant wild flowers. It is named for Queen Anne of England, who reigned from 1702 to 1714. She was apparently quite fond of wearing lace on her dresses. I can remember as a child being told the flower's name and being invited to look for the "little drop of blood in the middle of the lace" where Queen Anne is said to have pricked her finger. It was a good story, and that's all I knew about Queen Anne's lace until I began to grow vegetables.

If you break off one of the leaves of Queen Anne's lace and smell the broken end, you will be reminded of a familiar vegetable: the carrot. Queen Anne's lace smells so much like a carrot that you might be tempted to pull up the plant to see if there isn't a thick orange root at the bottom. Because this plant is so prolific, it can afford the impact of your investigations, so pull it up. All you will find is a skinny little off-white root that would never compete at a farmer's market.

But you were not deceived. Queen Anne's lace is actually the wild version of the plant that has been domesticated and refined for human consumption. The Latin name for the wild flower is *Daucus carota* and for the domestic carrot *Daucus carota sativa*. Some books omit the subspecies *sativa* and refer to both plants as *Daucus carota*.

One of the reasons we don't recognize the close relationship between the two plants is that they are biennials. That means it takes two growing seasons for them to reproduce. We are most familiar with Queen Anne's lace in its second season when it has sent up flower stalks and is ready to go to seed. The garden carrot, on the other hand, we harvest at the end of the first season, or perhaps very early in the second. Unless you have tried to produce your own carrot seed, you have probably never let a row of carrots complete its life cycle. You've probably never seen more than the leaves the plant sends up during its first year and, of course, the familiar orange root.

Queen Anne's lace and our domestic carrot are both members of the parsley family. This family also provides us with celery and parsnips, as well as many of our most aromatic herbs and seasonings—parsley, dill, caraway, fennel, coriander, cumin, and anise. Interestingly enough, this same family offers some very deadly poisons, including the hemlock that Socrates drank when he was condemned for corrupting the youth of Athens. This poison hemlock looks much like Queen Anne's lace, so you should avoid taste tests when you're examining this family of plants.

Some people consider Queen Anne's lace a weed rather than a wild flower. It can indeed spread over an abandoned field very quickly. If you pay close attention to what happens to the flower heads of Queen Anne's lace as the summer goes on, you'll see how strategically they prepare for the next generation.

During the summer numerous small flowers spread themselves out in the broad white medallion that gives the plant its common name. If you look closely at the flower head at this stage, you will see lots of small branches growing out of the main flower stalk, and yet more still smaller branches growing out of these first branches. Each of these incredibly small branches has an incredibly small five-petaled flower at its tip, and each small flower contributes to the symmetry of the whole. The flowers toward the center are the smallest, with the flowers around the outside stretching their outermost petals to relatively large sizes to give the flower head its round shape.

While you're studying the flower head, you'll probably notice the dark spot in the middle. I should mention it even if I can't explain it. This dark spot is a single floret growing from a single stalk. It is a mystery. No one seems to know why it's there or what it does. The folklore about that drop of Queen Anne's blood I learned as a child is the closest I've come to an explanation.

QUEEN ANNE'S LACE

If you smell the flowers of Queen Anne's lace, you may be surprised to discover that such a common weed smells so sweet. The aroma is part of its strategy. Many different insects are attracted to it. When they get to the flowers, they discover that the nectar is quite accessible, so Queen Anne's lace is quite popular among insects. The number of flowers and the numerous insects that visit the flowers assure a good rate of pollination, and Queen Anne's lace is well on its way to producing the next generation.

With such a flat, exposed flower head you'd think Queen Anne's lace might lose much of its pollen to rain, but the flower heads are careful to protect themselves until they've been pollinated. If a summer rain threatens, the horizontal flower head merely hangs itself vertically until the rain passes and then looks back up at the sun, inviting insects to return to their work.

After the flowers have been pollinated, the flat white "lace" curls inward to become a "bird's nest." Inside the "nest" hundreds of spiny little seeds develop. When the plant dries out and becomes brittle, the "bird's nest" sometimes breaks off and becomes a tumbleweed, which the wind then blows to another location. The seeds fall out of the "nest," and, if they land on suitable ground, they produce a new generation of Queen Anne's lace.

Familiar weeds and wild flowers offer some of the best opportunities to learn about nature. These plants are familiar because they are abundant, and their abundance is in turn testimony to their success. If we can look at a flower like Queen Anne's lace and learn about its adaptations and methods of survival, we can begin to understand something about the way nature does things—and perhaps appreciate the vulnerability of less prolific species like ourselves.

34

Cattails

I don't think of cattails as flowers, but they are indeed flowering plants with their own special methods of pollinating themselves and producing seeds. If we follow the annual cycle of the cattail from its first appearance at the beginning of the growing season to its retreat underground in the fall, we will see a plant that offers human beings a number of useful products as it proceeds with its own necessary business of growing and propagating itself.

The cattail is a perennial—it lives for several years. An annual, in contrast, has one brief season to germinate, grow, flower, produce seed, and die. Garden plants like green beans, tomatoes, squash, and pumpkins are annuals. A biennial takes two seasons to produce seed. It becomes dormant during the winter after its first growing season and comes back the next spring to finish its life cycle. By the end of its second season it has flowered and produced seed for the next generation. In our vegetable garden we allow such biennials as beets and carrots only the first year's worth of their life cycle.

A perennial stays alive for many years. It becomes dormant each winter, but it is ready for another growing season as soon as the lengthening days of spring break its dormancy. Trees and shrubs are perennials. In the vegetable garden asparagus and rhubarb are two familiar perennials.

The green cattail shoots you see pushing up through the mud early each spring are the first sign of the plant's renewed growth. They are also the cattail's first offering to human beings who might be hungry for fresh plant food after a long

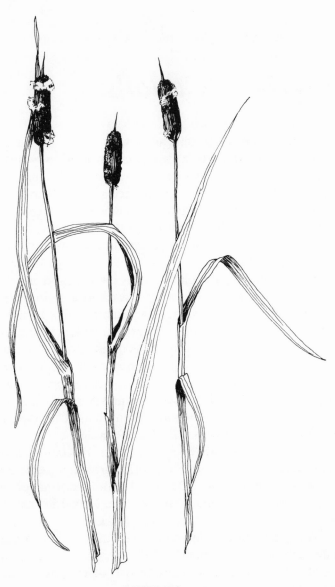

CATTAILS

winter of frozen, canned, or dried foods. You can pull the shoots from the mud, wash them, and eat them raw like celery or cooked like other vegetables. Cattails should be harvested as you would harvest asparagus: after your early pickings, leave them alone so that they can proceed to the later stages of their seasonal cycle. While they are growing you can still harvest an occasional plant and eat the tender white bottoms of the leaves the same way you ate the shoots.

As the summer goes on the cattails will send up their familiar flower stalks, which are entirely green at first. At the very top is a slender spike that holds the male flowers. I never noticed this structure until I started watching the cattail throughout the summer. The male flowers that grow on the spike will produce pollen to fertilize the female flowers that grow below them. The closely packed female flowers will become the familiar brown head later in the summer.

A protective green sheath covers the male flowers while they're maturing. When the pollen grains inside turn yellow, the male flower spike looks very much like a miniature ear of corn. Before the pollen dries and begins to sift down to pollinate the female flowers, you can break off the sheathed spikes and prepare them as you would corn on the cob. Or you can wait for the pollen to dry and use it as a flour supplement in breads, pancakes, and other baked goods. Cattail pollen also serves as a soup or stew thickener.

Because it takes many of these miniature "ears of corn" to make a meal and a large quantity of pollen to make a little bit of flour, treat yourself to these parts of the cattail sparingly. If you harvest all the pollen spikes on all the cattails, you're not leaving any pollen for the female flowers. The cattail is arranged to pollinate itself and, with the help of gentle breezes, its neighbors as well. If the pollen is gone, the cattail cannot proceed.

While the flower stalk occupies itself with flower, pollen, and seed production, the long slender leaves busily manufacture food for the entire plant. Although we cannot eat the leaves, they, too, have their use. They can be dried and then soaked in water to become pliant weaving material for chair seats and mats.

As if these offerings weren't enough, the cattail goes on producing additional useful products. In the fall you will see the brown heads turn to "cotton," consisting of thousands of little parachutes designed to carry cattail seeds away from the parent plant. Indians used this absorbent material to line their papoose carriers. It can also be used as insulation and pillow stuffing.

Finally, we come to the roots. In the fall, when the cattail prepares for its winter dormancy, the roots are full of starch. You can dig, clean, and boil them into a hearty soup or stew. Or you can dry them and grind them into flour.

I have heard about the possibility of commercial cattail farming, but I'd rather sustain a small-scale relationship with the wild cattails that grow near where I live. When I consider that the species produces numerous new plants every year, each one of which produces thousands of seeds for future generations, I feel that my random harvesting of a part here and a part there doesn't do much damage. But, as with all of nature's offerings, if I take too much, or if too many people each decide to take a little bit, we could affect even the prolific cattail's ability to perpetuate itself.

35

Slugs

Slugs are not snails that have crawled out of their shells. Nor are they the "bloodsuckers" many people seem to think they are. If you pick one up, you may at worst get some of the slug's protective mucus on your hands. The slug isn't the least bit interested in your blood, and, even if it were, it doesn't have the equipment to get at it.

The confusion between leeches and slugs has damaged the slug's reputation. The two animals do look somewhat alike—but only from a distance. If you look at both closely, you will notice obvious differences. The leech belongs to the phylum of animals called annelids, making it closer kin to the earthworm than the slug. It is a long, flat, segmented worm with specialized suckers at both ends of its body. The leech attaches itself to freshwater animals to suck their blood, and it will attach itself to a swimming or wading human being as readily as to an aquatic animal.

If you examine a slug, you will see that it has no segments—its body is all one piece. Turn it over and look at both ends of its body; you will see that it has no equipment for sucking. The slug's smooth, flat "foot" sticks to things by adhesion rather than by suction. Its tiny mouth, at the front end of its body, is designed to rasp away at vegetation. I don't think human skin, being tough and salty, would be at all tempting to a slug.

The slug belongs to a phylum of animals called mollusks. It is related to oysters, clams, squids, and octopi rather than to earthworms and leeches. Mollusks have soft, moist, unsegmented bodies. Within the phylum slugs fall into the class Gastropoda, which means "stomach-foot." Gastropods include all the snails and slugs—those which inhabit the oceans, those which live in fresh water, and those which live on land. Each has the characteristic "foot" on the underside of its body.

The confusion between slugs and snails is more natural than the confusion between slugs and leeches because they are alike in many ways. The slug has merely taken a slightly different evolutionary path from the snail. It has evolved away from the shell and apparently has had as much success without a shell as the snail has had with one.

Look closely at a slug's back and you will see a saddlelike growth of a texture different from the rest of its body. That's the mantle. Whereas the snail's mantle is always busy secreting calcium carbonate for the shell, the slug's mantle is nonfunctional. In some slugs there is a hard plate of calcareous material inside the mantle, but in most species the mantle is just extra padding on the slug's back.

You'd think that without a shell a slug would be at a disadvantage, but it seems to survive as well as a snail does. It is more vulnerable to weather because it can't withdraw into a shell and close the door behind it the way a snail can if the weather gets too dry. It just has to stay in a moist environment. It is also vulnerable to predators because it has no place to hide if it is caught out in the open. But actually a snail isn't much better off because a rodent can easily gnaw through its shell, or a bird can drop a snail from a height to smash the shell on a rock.

A slug feels moist to the touch because glands in its skin secrete mucus. This mucus helps the slug move. It slides along a track it lays down as it goes. The mucus also protects the slug's tender body from sharp obstacles it might encounter in its leisurely progress. In a laboratory experiment a researcher placed a razor blade upright in front of a slug. The slug proceeded to slip and slide its way right over the razor, its mucus protecting it from injury.

Some slugs are considered pests because they eat garden vegetables. The slugs that invade gardens are for the most part European and African imports. These imports tend to be colonial, gathering in great numbers to eat the plants we like to grow. Gardening books offer all kinds of home remedies for slug problems. Some suggest drowning them in beer. Others suggest sprinkling them with salt or lime.

Our native slugs don't cause much trouble. They are solitary and prefer wild vegetation or rotting organic matter to the edibles we cultivate. The slug I see most often in my part of Vermont is a native. It is about an inch long, is amber in color, and secretes an amber mucus. Its mantle covers only a small portion of its back. Up front are the four tentacles common to most snails and slugs. The longer upper tentacles have small eyes at their tips, and the slug swings them around like periscopes to examine its environment. The lower tentacles are feelers, which provide the slug with another way to explore its environment.

These slugs spend most of their time in the moist space under rotting logs. Recently I turned over a log in hopes of seeing a slug, and I discovered not only a slug but a small cluster of its eggs. They were little white spheres that looked as caviar might look if it were bleached white.

Native slugs play an important ecological role. As they eat they break down organic matter, which is important to soil formation. In turn, they are eaten and kept in check by birds, frogs, toads, salamanders, snakes, turtles, chipmunks, field mice, shrews, moles, and beetles.

The lesson to be learned from our experience with imported

slugs is that imported animals don't always fit into existing ecosystems. If we had left European and African slugs in their native habitats, we probably wouldn't consider slugs pests. Perhaps in time these imported slugs will find a place in our ecology. But with all our gardens and greenhouses, and high populations of imported slugs congregating, finding plenty of food, and reproducing themselves around these gardens and greenhouses, it's difficult for our resident slug-eaters to control their populations.

I am glad the small amber slug that inhabits my neighborhood is a native. It lives in the moist woods and feeds on decaying plant matter it finds there. It leaves my garden to me.

36

Centipedes and Millipedes

Many people mention centipedes and millipedes in the same breath as if the two were essentially the same animal with a different number of legs. From their names you might picture centipedes as creepy-crawlies with a hundred legs and millipedes as the same with a thousand legs. But their names are misleading and contribute to the confusion between these two very different animals. Both belong to the phylum Arthropoda, making them relatives of insects, spiders, and crustaceans. All arthropods have jointed legs, but centipedes and millipedes have more of them.

In general, millipedes have more legs than centipedes because millipedes have two pairs of legs per body segment while centipedes have only one pair. To that extent their names are not misleading. But millipedes never have a thousand legs, and centipedes often have more than a hundred. Furthermore, some species of centipedes have more legs than some species of millipedes. With approximately 200 species of centipedes in the United States and 150 species of millipedes, and leg counts ranging from 30 to over 300, counting the number of legs would be the most frustrating and least interesting way to distinguish the two animals. It might be better to begin with general appearance. Both animals have segmented bodies and jointed legs, but the centipede is flat and its legs are long. The millipede looks more like a worm—its body is cylindrical and its legs are short.

The different body shapes and leg lengths reflect the different lives the two animals live. The centipede, with its long legs, can move quite fast. Its flat body enables it to crawl into cracks and under things. The centipede needs its speed and maneuverability because it is a predator. It eats insects, slugs, earthworms, and other small animals that share the dark, moist places it inhabits. An additional adaptation also marks it as a predator: the pair of legs on the first body segment are not walking legs but poison "claws." With these specialized appendages the centipede injects its prey with a paralyzing fluid that makes the prey easier to manage.

The short-legged, slow-moving, wormlike millipede is a vegetarian. It lives for the most part on dead and decaying plant matter. Because its food sources neither run away nor put up a fight, it has no need for speed or special weapons. The millipede's weapons are weapons of defense. When attacked, it curls up so that its hard back protects its legs and soft underparts. It can also make itself obnoxious by excreting a substance from stink glands along its sides.

Another distinction between these two distant cousins is their living arrangements. The millipede prefers leaf litter and the top few inches of soil, where it finds plenty of decaying plant food. It sometimes digs deeper in search of moisture. The centipede, on the other hand, likes the spaces under bark and beneath stones, where it finds the invertebrates it preys on. It has also been known to inhabit moist basements.

The house centipede is a special case. Whereas other centipedes are strictly nocturnal and have poor eyesight, the house centipede hunts during the day and has compound eyes quite similar to an insect's. Although the presence of thirty-legged house centipedes in your basement might disconcert you, it's actually an advantage to have them there because they prey on insects.

Although both centipedes and millipedes may be repulsive

to you when you first see them, if you can understand the important roles they are playing, perhaps you can learn to live with them—even the centipedes in your basement. The millipede is highly beneficial because it contributes to the ongoing process of soil building. By eating and digesting dead vegetation, it breaks plant matter down into the simple elements that plants still alive and growing require. The centipedes are performing an equally important function as insect and slug controls.

Whatever damage either of these animals may do to living plants or beneficial insects must be weighed against their positive contributions. In pursuing their own quiet lives in the dark, moist, and hidden places they prefer, centipedes and millipedes help nature maintain its balances and recycle its life-supporting resources.

37

Shrews

What is the smallest living mammal? Which mammal, not counting the pouched marsupials, is the most ancient? The answer to both these questions is the shrew. Your next question probably is, What's a shrew? Shakespeare wrote about taming one, but she wasn't especially small, and the species she belonged to isn't especially ancient.

Interestingly enough, the modern word *shrew* with its meaning of an ill-tempered and scolding woman had its origin in the word the Anglo-Saxons used to refer to the animals, but not because the animal was ill-tempered and scolding. To an Anglo-Saxon *screawa* meant a venomous animal. When applied to a person it meant wicked and malicious. In Middle English the word became *shrew*. It still meant wicked and malicious, but it began to be applied especially to women—specifically the ill-tempered and scolding type that Shakespeare characterized. The same word also evolved into our modern adjective *shrewd*, which as far as I can tell applies equally to men and women.

What kind of animal is it that gave Anglo-Saxons *screawa* and us the modern *shrew* and *shrewd*? It's a nervous little mammal that spends most of its brief life hiding under leaf litter or in tunnels under ground. Most people have never seen one. Or they may have caught only a brief glimpse of one scurrying from one hiding place to another and thought it was a mouse. If they had had a chance to look more closely, however, they would have seen a very pointed snout. Further examination would have revealed numerous other differences in eyes, ears, teeth, paws, fur, and tail to clearly distinguish the shrew from a mouse.

The venom referred to in the meaning of the original Anglo-Saxon word is poisonous saliva produced by glands in a shrew's lower jaw. While in most species the poison is very weak, the short-tail shrew's poison is strong enough to kill a mouse. It's not strong enough to harm a human being, but it can stupefy a mouse and cause convulsions.

The short-tail shrew is about the same size as a house mouse, but its body is more cylindrical, its tail is shorter and hairier, it has no external ears, its eyes are so small that they're hardly visible, and it's darker in color. Also, while the house mouse has chisel-like front teeth adapted to gnawing plant food, a shrew has sharp, pointed teeth suitable for eating insects, other small invertebrates, and even mice.

The short-tail shrew is common in the Northeast. Four species of shrews that are smaller than the short-tail shrew also inhabit this area. The pygmy shrew is the smallest mammal in the Western Hemisphere. It is about two inches long and weighs about as much as a dime. I've never seen a pygmy shrew, but I've seen the masked shrew, which is the next smallest. It was small enough to convince me that the pygmy shrew must be very small indeed. The masked shrew I saw had drowned in one of our sap buckets during sugaring. Its body was about the size of my thumb, complete with a tiny pointed snout, delicate little feet, and a hairy tail over an inch long. I haven't seen the other small shrews—the smoky and the long-tail. I don't think I'll ever see them unless I take up live-trapping.

A sixth shrew is about the same size as the short-tail shrew but has a longer tail. This northern water shrew differs from the others in that it prefers an aquatic environment. It has special hairs on its hind feet that adapt it for swimming. It is often found along streams or in other wet places.

All shrews are voracious insect eaters. They have such a high rate of metabolism that they need to eat almost constantly to stay alive. If deprived of food for more than a few hours, some species will die of starvation. Many shrews eat more than their own weight in food each day, and the little masked shrew has been credited with eating more than three times its weight in a day. Because shrews need to eat so much and so often, they can't sleep for very long at a stretch. Instead, they grab short naps between meals. Otherwise, they are busy getting food twenty-four hours a day, four seasons of the year.

Although I've never seen a live shrew up close, I frequently find dead shrews—short-tails—when I'm walking in the woods. The body is always intact. Shrews have scent glands in their hind flanks that exude a strong, musky odor, and this odor is so offensive to most predators that after they've killed a shrew they leave it to decompose on the forest floor. Only hawks and owls, which do not have an appreciable sense of smell, eat the shrews they catch.

These tiny, high-intensity creatures, with a history that goes back to the earliest fossil records of mammals, are easier to read about than to see. But knowing how active shrews must be to survive, I always keep an eye open for one when I'm walking near a place where shrews might live.

38

Ladybugs

Ladybugs are among our best friends. Insects are so easily thought of as pests and bothers that it's fortunate we have at least one familiar insect that frequently comes to our rescue. Ladybugs have demonstrated time and again the beneficial effects insects can have.

In the late 1880s, for instance, a destructive insect called the cottony cushion scale was accidentally transported from Australia to California. It threatened to destroy the entire citrus crop there. In Australia the cottony cushion scale had a natural enemy—a species of ladybug. So we imported some of these Australian ladybugs to battle the citrus-destroying pests, and the ladybugs won.

Long before the 1880s, European farmers had noticed that ladybugs ate harmful insects. Their very name comes from the medieval habit of referring to them as "Our Lady's beetle." The ladybug's reputation has always been good, but it has gotten even better as biological controls of insect pests have begun to prove more effective than chemical controls. In California people climb the mountains each fall and gather great masses of ladybugs that have been hiding up there in caves during the hot summer months. They preserve these ladybugs over the winter and then market them to farmers and orchardists early in the spring. About 30,000 ladybugs will protect 10 acres.

Ladybugs are among the first insects a child learns about. When parents see one, they recite the familiar nursery rhyme:

> Ladybug, ladybug,
> Fly away home,
> Your house is on fire,
> And your children will burn.

While based on truth, the rhyme is also misleading. It refers to the English custom of burning hop vines after the harvest to get rid of insect pests. Unfortunately, where there are insect pests there are also ladybugs and their larvae because both feed on insect pests. And because ladybug larvae can't fly, burning vines mean burning larvae.

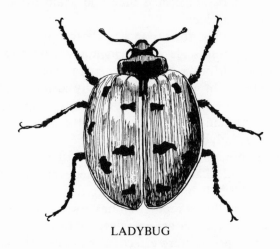

LADYBUG

The nursery rhyme is misleading, however, because it implies that parent ladybugs have an interest in their offspring. They don't. The female lays her eggs where the young are likely to find insect food, but that is the extent of her concern. Once the eggs are laid the mother is off to worry about her next meal, her next mate, and her next batch of eggs.

The ladybug's life cycle is typical of insects that have a

complete metamorphosis. The adult female lays her eggs on the leaves of a plant that is appealing to aphids and scale insects. After about five days the eggs hatch into voracious larvae that look more like caterpillars than beetles. These larvae eat and grow for two to three weeks, shedding their skin four times before they're ready to begin pupation, the third stage of their lives. During pupation they rest in the shelter of the old skin for about six days. Finally, they emerge as adult ladybugs. Because the whole four-stage life cycle takes only a few weeks, several generations of ladybugs are born during the warm months of summer.

In addition to a high birth rate, ladybugs also enjoy a reasonably good survival rate. Bright coloration is often a warning to predators that the brightly colored animal doesn't taste good. The ladybug's reddish color is therefore protective. If a predator ignores the color and attacks anyway, the ladybug plays dead, which makes it unappealing to predators that like live food. If the predator still persists, the ladybug emits a foul-smelling fluid from its thorax and from between the segments of its legs.

In the fall adult ladybugs gather in groups and seek safe places for hibernation. They usually choose loose bark, rotting logs, or rock crevices, but occasionally they will work their way into a house. If they do, consider them a good omen for next year.

39

Hawks

It amazes me how many animals have bad reputations not because of what they do but because of what human beings think they do. We sometimes jump to conclusions about one species from the behavior of another species. We frequently choose to believe rumor, gossip, and exaggeration rather than to observe animal behavior closely. Along with bees, wasps, snakes, and spiders, hawks suffer from the negative images human beings impose on them—images that would be corrected readily if people would only give individual hawks the benefit of the doubt and watch what they do.

In the case of hawks, the confusion about behavior is compounded by a confusion in nomenclature that developed when English-speaking colonists came to the New World in the 1600s and 1700s. In England only one group of predatory birds were—and still are—called *hawks.* Those birds belong to the genus *accipiter,* and they eat other birds. Unfortunately, the American colonists applied the word *hawk* and its meaning "bird eater" to most of the curved-beaked, strong-taloned, daytime predators they saw. Only our goshawks, sharp-shinned hawks, and Cooper's hawks are true hawks, or *accipiters*.

Hawks belonging to the genus *buteo*, which includes our broad-winged, red-tailed, red-shouldered, and rough-legged "hawks," have taken the greatest beating. These birds prefer to eat rodents, insects, amphibians, and reptiles, yet they are looked upon as ruthless bird-eaters because they carry the name *hawk*.

To revert to the English nomenclature would only confuse Americans further, however, because the English call their buteos *buzzards*, and Americans use the word *buzzard* to refer to vultures. Vultures differ from both accipiters and buteos in that they don't eat live prey at all. They live on carrion—dead flesh. The buteos are caught in a language trap. If we call them *hawks* they're bird killers; if we call them *buzzards* they're garbage collectors. Could it be that a return to Latin is the only way for twentieth-century Americans to clear the reputations of their buteos?

The problem between human beings and accipiters arose in the first place because some of the birds accipiters prey on are domestic or game species. Bird-eating hawks don't make the same distinctions human beings make—or maybe they do, preferring to eat some of the same birds we like to eat. They just don't honor what we have come to think of as our prior claim. A bird is a bird, and if it is available to be eaten a hawk that is hungry will eat it, whatever its value to human beings. Actually accipiters eat more small birds than chickens or game birds, but their occasional raids on the chicken yard or on birds that human beings are saving to hunt and eat themselves have gained them (and by linguistic confusion, the buteos) a notoriety difficult to dispel.

The irony—and even tragedy—of this battle between human beings and hawks is that the farmer who's angry because some hawk ate his chickens, or a hunter who's angry because some hawk ate a game bird, will most likely kill a bird innocent of the deed. Unfortunately, buteos are more visible than accipiters. They soar in great lazy circles in the sky, or they perch on fence posts or in treetops. They are waiting for insects, rodents, and other small animals to reveal themselves. The accipiters, on the other hand, usually hide in a wooded area, well covered, as they wait to spot the birds they prey on. The angry farmer who strings dead hawks along his fence as a misguided warning to bird eaters has usually destroyed a number of innocent buteos that would have helped him by eating insects, rats, and mice. Meanwhile, the accipiter that killed his chickens is probably still in the woods, waiting for another chance.

RED-TAILED
HAWK

Perhaps the best way to clear the various hawks' reputations is with statistics. The United States Department of Agriculture conducted studies to examine the stomach contents of 5,185 hawks to determine what they had eaten and in what proportions. Here is what they learned:

ACCIPITERS

Cooper's hawk:	55.0% small birds
	17.0% rats and mice
	12.0% game birds
	10.0% poultry
	3.3% insects
	1.7% rabbits
	1.0% frogs, etc.
Sharp-shinned hawk:	96.4% small birds
	2.6% rats, etc.
	.7% insects
	.1% frogs
	.1% rabbits
	.1% poultry

BUTEOS

Broad-winged hawk:	39.7% insects
	30.9% frogs and snakes
	23.0% rats and mice
	3.4% small birds
	2.0% aquatic animals
	.5% game birds
	.5% rabbits
Red-shouldered hawk:	32.0% insects
	28.0% rats and mice
	25.0% frogs and snakes
	5.3% aquatic animals
	6.5% small birds
	1.4% poultry
	.9% game birds
	.9% rabbits

Red-tailed hawk:	55.0% rats and mice
	10.5% insects
	9.3% rabbits and squirrels
	9.2% small birds
	6.3% poultry
	6.1% frogs and snakes
	2.1% game birds
	1.5% aquatic animals
Rough-legged hawk:	72.0% rats and mice
	8.6% rabbits and squirrels
	6.5% insects
	4.3% small birds
	4.3% game birds
	2.2% aquatic animals
	2.1% frogs and snakes

Given the low percentages for poultry and game birds and the high percentages for rodents and insects, it's to our advantage to let all the hawks—both buteos and accipiters—go about their business according to their dietary inclinations.

Hawk identification takes a while, but buteos can be distinguished from accipiters fairly easily. Accipiters have short, round wings and a long tail. Their typical flight pattern is several quick beats followed by a glide. They are woodland birds adapted for the dodging and darting necessary to maneuver among trees and branches in pursuit of their prey. The buteos, on the other hand, have broad wings and a broad, rounded tail that enable them to soar in wide circles high in the open sky. Their keen eyesight detects even the slightest motion in the fields and meadows below.

Making the distinction between accipiters and buteos is just a start. Further identification of the different species that nest near you or pass through in migration takes time, patience, a good pair of binoculars, and eyes you have trained to look for colors and patterns of white.

Another predatory bird that we call a *hawk* the English call a *harrier*. Its common name in this country is the marsh hawk. Marsh is descriptive of where you may see it, but *hawk* again is misleading because it eats as many rodents and insects as it eats birds.

Finally, you may see huge vultures circling overhead. Vultures, which belong to the same order as all these other birds, perform a service quite different from the others' pest control. Their job is to clean up the environment by removing the flesh of dead animals.

Law now protects all predatory birds. It is illegal to shoot them, whatever damage you think they might be doing. Because predators—both birds and other animals—have been among the most misunderstood and abused of the wild animals with whom we share this earth, it has become necessary to protect them legally to assure ourselves ecological balance.

There is nothing romantic or fuzzy-headed about protecting predators. If we kill hawks to protect poultry and game birds, we invite insect and rodent populations to expand. The long-term effects of these exchanges are difficult to predict mathematically and impossible to resolve economically or ethically. Therefore, we'd best align our human laws with the laws of nature. We should spend less time worrying about the supposed damage wild animals are doing and more time looking for our own proper place in the scheme of things.

Fall and
Winter Again

40

Earthworms

When I dig potatoes in the fall, I feel guilty about this one last intrusion on the earthworms. All spring and summer I have been disturbing their peace—rototilling, planting, weeding, thinning, harvesting, uprooting, digging, and walking around in the garden. It's a wonder the earthworms stay around. But they do because I feed them well, adding manure, compost, leaves, and other organic matter to the soil every chance I get.

Everyone knows what an earthworm looks like, but there are some features that may have escaped the casual observer's attention. An adult earthworm can be up to 11 inches long with 100–200 body segments. Between the 32nd and 37th body segments is an enlarged area called the clitellum. It produces extra mucus that aids in reproduction. If the body is severed behind the clitellum, the earthworm can grow a new tail; but if it is severed in front of the clitellum, the earthworm will die.

Each body segment has four pairs of bristlelike structures called setae. They help the earthworm move and climb and cling to its burrow. If you've ever watched a robin tug on an earthworm, you've seen the setae in action. They are all the earthworm has for defense, and it uses them to hang onto the inside of its burrow for dear life.

Besides robins—and human beings, with their careless spades, trowels, hoes, rototillers, and designs on worms for fish bait—earthworms have a number of other threats to contend with. Their predators include woodcocks, toads, frogs, snakes, turtles, skunks, some slugs, some beetles, centipedes, shrews, and moles. In an attempt to avoid some of these predators, and also to avoid drying out in the hot sun, earthworms are adapted to nighttime activity.

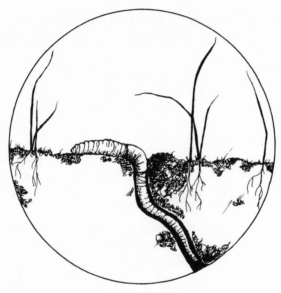

EARTHWORM

The only time you see an earthworm above the surface in daylight is when you turn it up in soil you're digging, or when a heavy rain has flooded it out of its burrow. An earthworm doesn't have eyes, but it has light-sensitive cells on the top of its body near its head. These cells tell it to go back underground when daylight—or the beam of a flashlight— hits them.

As with all animals, much of an earthworm's activity involves food-getting. All night long an earthworm eats away at whatever it finds on the surface of the soil. It is not choosy. It will eat either plant or animal debris, but its favorite food is rotting vegetation.

It also eats a lot of soil. An earthworm digs by eating the soil it can't push out of its way. Everything the earthworm ingests undergoes significant changes as it works through the digestive system. The gizzard grinds up particles of soil into smaller pieces. Nutrients are absorbed in the intestine, and everything else, including intestinal fluids and pulverized soil, is excreted. The worm deposits its wastes, which are called castings, in the topsoil and on the surface of the ground above its burrow.

These castings are little deposits of well-mixed and reconditioned soil. One casting isn't much, but the many castings of the many earthworms that inhabit a healthy soil make a difference. Darwin devoted 40 years of research and observation to the earthworm. Working from an estimated 53,767 earthworms per acre of garden soil, he calculated that about half that number, or 26,886, might inhabit old pasture soil. In a year these 26,886 earthworms would bring about 15 tons of soil to the surface in their castings. In 10 years they would add a layer of about two inches of reconditioned soil.

In addition to eating, burrowing, and reconditioning the soil in the process, the earthworm also has to reproduce to assure the continuation of the species. Each earthworm has both male and female organs, which you'd think would make reproduction extremely simple. But an earthworm doesn't fertilize its own eggs with its own sperm; it exchanges sperm with another earthworm.

Two earthworms mate by lying head to tail with their front undersides pressed close together. Sperm travels from the 15th segment of one to special storage sacs in the 9th and 10th segments of the other. After exchanging sperm the two earthworms separate.

When the eggs are ready to be fertilized the earthworm's clitellum secretes a girdle of mucus, which will become a protective cocoon for the eggs. As the earthworm pushes this girdle off over its head, the mucus gathers up eggs from segment 14 and stored sperm from segments 9 and 10. When the girdle slips off over the earthworm's head, both ends close to form a snug cocoon where the fertilized eggs can grow into new little earthworms.

In winter earthworms go deeper underground. They burrow beneath the frost line and spend the winter in an inactive state. They are probably happier down there where they aren't bothered by me and the other surface creatures that torment—or eat—them. They still have hungry moles and shrews to contend with, but I'm confident nature has arranged things so that at least some earthworms will return next spring to eat and mate and help me with my garden.

41

Nocturnal Animals

Daytime nature walks are good exercise, but if you want to see animals in action, take your walks at dawn or dusk—or you might even go outdoors at midnight once in a while. Many animals have developed a definite preference for darkness.

Animals that prefer night have good reasons for their preference. Some like night because there is less competition for a shared food supply. Owls, for instance, search for prey at night while hawks search during the day, thus avoiding direct competition. Others prefer night because they feel safer when it's dark.

Whatever their reasons for being active at night, most nocturnal animals have adaptations that specially equip them for food getting and self-protection in the dark. Two of the best known and best adapted nocturnal animals are bats and owls. The former is a small insect-eating mammal that is confusing to people because it flies like a bird. The latter is a bird of prey that strikes terror into the hearts of small rodents and can even send a chill down the human spine with a screech or hoot from the dark woods.

The bat has evolved a unique system of echolocation. It bounces high frequency sound waves off objects around it and finds what it's looking for—or avoids what it doesn't want to hit—by listening to the returning sound waves. This highly developed sound system makes highly developed night sight unnecessary. The bat does have eyes, but the eyes can't see very far, nor can they perceive stationary objects.

Owls don't have echolocation like bats, but they do have excellent hearing that helps them hunt at night. Their ears are widely spaced, and their ear flaps are slightly asymmetrical, which apparently helps owls locate the exact place a sound is coming from. Ornithologists theorize that the owl's broad facial disc also contributes to precise sound reception. Carefully controlled experiments have shown that some owls can strike their prey in complete darkness. Hearing apparently plays a more important role than seeing in the success of at least some owls as night hunters.

Owls also have large, light-sensitive eyes, so they can see quite well in very little light. Their binocular vision gives them good depth perception, and their mobile necks enable them to direct their binocular vision at objects to the left or right.

Another adaptation to life in the dark is the owl's ability to descend on its prey silently. Its primary feathers have soft edges, so there is no sound of air rushing through wings to alert an animal to the owl's presence. Because nocturnal animals are very sensitive to sound, the owl's silence is necessary to its success as a nocturnal predator.

When I think of other animals I see at night, I picture eyes that glow in the dark. That's because I am usually driving when I see them, and my headlights, which are my adaptation to the night, shine straight into their eyes. The glow that seems to be coming from some deep-burning inner fire is actually coming from mirror-like reflectors that line the backs of nocturnal animals' eyes.

These reflectors are a special adaptation. They bounce light back from behind the retina to give the retina a second chance to absorb it. In dim light this double chance at what little light is available is a definite advantage. The glowing eyes I see most often belong to cats, raccoons, porcupines, skunks, and deer.

Other animals that prefer night to day include rabbits, deer mice, and flying squirrels. These small animals have so many predators that they have learned to take advantage of whatever protection darkness may provide. They also have so many daytime relatives that they probably have better luck with food-getting at night while many of their cousins are sleeping.

Finally, there are the beavers. Whereas they are not truly nocturnal animals in the same way that the well-adapted bats and owls are, beavers have adapted to a nighttime existence the same way that human beings who happen to work the night shift have. Both are capable of changing their habits to work at night and sleep during the day. Beavers have become night workers in response to human presence. They have learned to feed and perform repairs at night when human beings are not around, and they sleep during the day in the safety of their well-built lodges.

Human beings, who are essentially daytime creatures, dominate only part of each 24-hour period. In the competition for food and space that has shaped the evolutionary patterns of plants and animals, many organisms have learned to live in darkness, when daytime species like ourselves are sound asleep.

42

Chipmunks

Chipmunks are familiar to everyone. Although they are like squirrels in some ways, they also have interesting characteristics of their own. When I think about the numerous chipmunks I see in the woods around my house, my first thought is that they're prettier than squirrels. They are also smaller, more numerous, and more readily seen than red or gray squirrels.

We see chipmunks more readily because they are ground dwellers. Instead of climbing trees and leaping from branch to branch high above our heads, they scurry around on the forest floor. Instead of living in a tree house, they live in an underground burrow.

The chipmunk's burrow is more than a place to hide from human beings and predators. It's a whole underground world where the chipmunk has provided space for everything it needs. One of a young chipmunk's first chores when it leaves its mother is to dig its own burrow.

It begins by digging a tunnel straight down into the earth, usually in a place that's protected or hidden by a log, stump, or boulder. After the initial drop, it digs at an angle until it is well below the frost line.

Then it digs the storage chambers, where it will store as much as half a bushel of nuts and seeds to see it through the winter. In addition to the storage chambers, it needs a sleeping chamber, a toilet chamber, and an exit tunnel. If the chipmunk happens to be a female, she will also dig a nest chamber somewhere near the center of this underground system.

Once the chipmunk has finished its excavations and emerged from its exit tunnel, it frequently goes back to the original entrance where it pushed out all the earth. It spreads this loose earth around so that there is nothing to alert a predator to the location of its home.

The chipmunk sometimes even plugs the original entrance and camouflages all signs of construction by spreading leaves and twigs over its work. The exit, which was dug from below and therefore has no tell-tale signs of excavation, becomes the sole access to the chipmunk's underground home.

While gray squirrels are busily burying their single acorns here and there for the long winter that lies ahead, and red squirrels are stashing their winter supplies in various safe places, the chipmunk is busily gathering nuts and seeds and bringing them back to its burrow. Its special cheek pouches save it from having to make a separate trip with each item of food. Surprising quantities of nuts and seeds can fit into these expandable cheeks. A chipmunk with its cheek pouches loaded looks as if it has a severe case of the mumps.

In its adaptation to winter, the chipmunk is midway between the hibernating woodchucks, which sleep through winter, living off their stored body fat, and the squirrels, which have to scurry around all winter to relocate their stored food supplies. The chipmunk, having carefully stored nonperishable food items in the storage chamber of its burrow, withdraws underground when winter comes and sleeps a good bit of the time. But it never goes into the deep sleep of hibernation, and therefore it has to maintain its bodily processes by feeding itself from its supply of stored food.

The chipmunk's life is not as snug and secure as the image of the well-supplied burrow suggests. It's only the lucky ones that survive to get their burrows dug and food gathered for winter. Chipmunks are relatively safe from predators when they're underground, but they have to spend much of the summer and fall above ground, feeding and gathering food for winter. Being small animals, somewhere between mice and rabbits in size, many chipmunks fall prey to hungry carnivores. Among the chipmunk's enemies are hawks, weasels, foxes, bears, fishers, bobcats, martens, lynxes, minks, coyotes, and snakes—not to mention domestic cats and speeding cars.

Despite the chipmunk's perilous existence, it seems to be a cheerful animal. It's one of the prettiest to look at, with its stripes and tans and reddish hues. I am fascinated by watching a chipmunk eating seeds or corn, or cramming food into its fat cheeks. In its busy preparations for winter the chipmunk is a model of Yankee industry and foresight.

The chipmunk is a great friend to the beginning naturalist. It's a wild animal that partakes of all the habits and characteristics of a life in the wild, but it is almost as familiar as a domestic cat or dog. Of all the wildlife that we know is out there, the chipmunk is one of the generous creatures that lets itself be seen.

43

Hares

For a few weeks toward the end of the summer, I saw the same hare almost every day. One of my favorite walks must have cut through its territory because I always saw it in the same place. It seemed to station itself at the foot of a hill, where it would wait until I was almost upon it. Then it would bound off into the woods.

Perhaps it was curious about me, or perhaps it was young and didn't know enough to fear human beings yet. Whatever its reasons for hanging around in the late summer, it's no longer at its station. I hope its curiosity and lack of caution didn't lead to its demise.

This large brown hare had big ears, big hind legs, and a body that would have made a hungry predator drool. It was a bigger animal than the generalized "rabbits" and "bunnies" I had in my imagination from children's stories. Actually, hares and rabbits are distinctly different animals. They belong to the same family, but hares belong to one genus and Old World and New World rabbits belong to two others. Hares are generally bigger than rabbits, and their young are born furred and open-eyed. Rabbits bear naked, blind, and helpless young.

The official name for the hare that spent the late summer near my house is *Lepus americanus,* but most people call it by one of its common names: the varying hare, the snowshoe hare, or the snowshoe rabbit. Fall is a good time to look for a varying hare because in fall it is in the process of "varying."

It undergoes a gradual molt that turns its summer brown fur to winter white. While it's changing color it's mottled, with patches of both colors showing.

Both the brown and white are protective colors. They match the seasonal background. It's almost impossible for predators to see a stationary hare. This protective coloration, however, is only part of the varying hare's strategy. If a predator comes too close, the hare can leap away quite suddenly. Once in motion, it can sustain a high rate of speed for a greater distance than many predators. It is also adept at dodging and circling to frustrate whatever animal is chasing it.

In addition to its protective coloration, speed, and stamina, the varying hare has another helpful adaptation. In winter it grows extra hair on its large hind feet to help support its weight in deep snow. Instead of having to strap on snowshoes as a human being would, the varying hare merely spreads its toes, and it is able to bound across the snow.

Despite their impressive adaptations, many hares fall victim to predators—including human beings and their dogs and cats. Among the hares' wild predators are bobcats, Canada lynx, coyotes, fishers, marten, mink, weasels, red foxes, great horned owls, and hawks.

The varying hare is active all year, changing its eating patterns with the seasons. In summer it thrives on grasses, green leaves, buds, and twigs. It drinks dew for water. In winter it eats the needles and twigs of conifers and the bark, buds, and twigs of aspen, maple, apple, and birch. It eats snow for water.

Like all preyed-upon species, the varying hare has an awesome capacity for reproduction. A pair left to their own devices could produce millions of descendents in just a few years. Because most hares don't live for many mating seasons, however, and because many of the young are eaten by predators before they are old enough to mate, this projection is no cause for immediate alarm. If something happened to the hare's predators, though, we would have a serious problem to contend with.

The varying hare's breeding season lasts from March to September. Gestation takes about thirty-seven days. The male is indifferent to the young, but he's interested in the female again within hours after she has had her litter. With such efficiency the female can potentially produce five litters in a breeding season, but three litters is closer to the average, with two to four young in each. The baby hares, called leverets, are more precocious than many mammal babies. They may begin hopping around within hours of their birth.

When I think of hare babies, I find myself trying to think of children's stories about hares. Most of the famous children's stories seem to be about European rabbits like Beatrix Potter's Flopsy, Mopsy, Cottontail, and Peter, or American cottontails like Joel Chandler Harris's Brer Rabbit and Thornton Burgess's Peter Rabbit. The only hare story I can think of is Aesop's fable about the tortoise and the hare. I don't know why hares don't have more stories, but they may be better off without them. I found myself fascinated by the real hare I saw and didn't have to correct for false impressions a story might have planted in my mind.

44

Woolly Bears

According to folklore, the hairy little caterpillar called the woolly bear is a weather prophet. The width of the rust-brown band around its middle is supposed to tell us what kind of winter to expect. A broad band means a mild winter; a narrow band means winter with a vengeance.

I can understand why human beings look to animals for signs at this time of year. Winter threatens us, and we'd like to foresee its force. If we could know in advance how long it was going to last and how cold it was going to be, we wouldn't feel so powerless against what lies ahead.

But animals have no clearer indication than we do of what the future holds. When winter arrives, we're all in it together. Human beings dress up more warmly and grit their teeth against the cold. Woolly bears, with their broad or narrow bands, crawl into what they hope is a safe place under leaves, debris, or grass and become inactive for the long months until spring.

Actually, the width of the woolly bear's brown band tells us more about the woolly bear than about the coming winter. A young woolly bear has more black than brown. As it grows, the brown band widens. An early winter sets younger woolly bears scurrying for shelter ahead of schedule. Perhaps that's how the narrow band has come to be associated with a long winter. But it's important to recognize that the woolly bear is not forecasting the future. Rather, it is responding to cold weather in the present.

If you find a woolly bear curled up under something at this time of year, you can pick it up gently. In response to the warmth of your hand, it will uncurl. This familiar caterpillar is in the second and longest stage of the four-stage life cycle of an insect called the Isabella tiger moth. The first stage of this moth's life cycle was the egg from which the woolly bear hatched. The young caterpillar ate green plants and grew during the late summer and fall. About now it is looking for a safe place to hide and become inactive for the winter months.

When the caterpillar reactivates in the spring, it will wander around for a while, eating and looking for a good place to pupate. It will then spin a cocoon out of silk and hair from its own body and enter the third stage of its life cycle. After a period of rest and physical change, the former woolly bear will emerge from the cocoon in late May as an adult Isabella tiger moth. It is the business of this adult to lay or fertilize eggs for the next generation. The female moth lays her eggs on a green plant that will provide food for the young woolly bears when they hatch during the summer.

In addition to entering the appropriate stages of its life cycle at appropriate times of year, the Isabella tiger moth has other adaptations that have helped it survive. The caterpillar's hairiness protects it from many predators. When anything threatens a woolly bear, it curls up and plays dead, presenting nothing but hairs to a would-be predator. Although the hairs are harmless, many animals don't like to eat hairy caterpillars. The skunk, however, is one predator that is not daunted. It rolls the woolly bear on the ground until the hairs fall off and then eats the defenseless caterpillar.

Next summer's Isabella tiger moth will be just another nocturnal moth that beats itself against your porch light, but the woolly bear caterpillar that roams the fields and roads in the fall is well known to everyone. As the familiar woolly

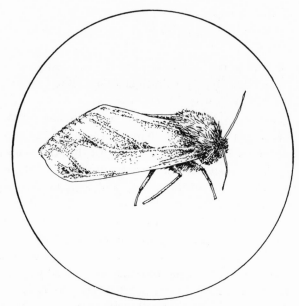

ISABELLA TIGER MOTH

bear disappears for winter, we humans have to ready ourselves for the season, too. Whether or not the woolly bear is a prophet, its well-furred little body crawling across the road on a crisp fall day is a harbinger of the cold weather that lies ahead.

45

Butternuts

Two years ago I discovered hundreds of butternuts beneath some butternut trees that grow in the woods nearby. In a burst of enthusiasm I gathered several buckets of them and spread them out in a back closet to dry. I forgot about them until a few weeks ago.

The nice thing about forgotten butternuts is that they are indestructible. Their tough shells are mouseproof, temperatureproof, humidityproof, insectproof, and, as far as I can tell, timeproof. Shells are designed to protect the germ of life, and the butternut shell does an exceptionally good job.

Some of my butternuts had already been invaded by moisture or insects when they were outdoors, and these, of course, did not survive the long indoor storage. But most of the nuts I opened in a delayed celebration of my harvest yielded rich, healthy nut meats.

A thick green outer husk covers the butternuts when they first fall from the trees. This fuzzy, sticky covering leaves a yellow-orange stain on your fingers if you rub it or try to remove it. After the nut has been on the ground for a while, the husk turns brown and decomposes. When I discovered my butternuts they were already dark brown and well camouflaged amidst the leaf litter of the forest floor.

Now, after the long dry months indoors, the outer husk had turned brittle. It flaked off in my fingers. The shell, however, was another story. The long storage had not weakened it. A butternut shell looks somewhat like a peach pit but has sharp ridges rather than holes. It is strong like a peach pit, too.

First, I attacked it with a nutcracker, but as hard as I could press the shell wouldn't yield. Next, I tried a hammer. With the first few taps the hammer bounced right off the shell, but finally the shell gave way.

Inside the resistant shell is a very delicious nut. It tastes like a strong, buttery walnut. The butternut is in fact a close relative of the easy-to-crack English walnut that you buy at the grocery store. It's more tightly packed, however, and the interior construction is much stronger. If you cut a thin cross section of the butternut with a hacksaw and remove the pieces of nut, you can study the substantial and unexpectedly beautiful inner structure. Craftspeople make jewelry out of these small samples of nature's artwork.

Despite the butternut's almost indestructible shell, individual nuts that find themselves in the right conditions germinate quite readily. A butternut left in the leaf litter, trampled into the forest floor, or perhaps buried by a provident but forgetful squirrel is subject to different influences than the butternuts I stored in my dry, seasonless, indoor closet.

Time, moisture, and temperature set many important natural processes in motion. In the spring moisture works through the protective butternut shell into the seed, and the swelling seed then bursts the shell with all the effortlessness of a natural event. So much for hammers . . .

I'm sure lots of animals besides human beings would like to eat butternuts, but few have the equipment to get through the shells. The red squirrel is the only wild animal I know of that has teeth strong enough to gnaw through a butternut shell. On a recent walk I discovered a squirrel-eaten butternut beside the trail. The squirrel had gnawed a large, irregular

U-shaped hole in the shell and neatly extricated the morsels of nut from the two main chambers. The red squirrel, with its small but well-adapted teeth, was much tidier in its work than I was with my ill-adapted hammer.

Some years are better than others for nut crops. The year I collected my butternuts was excellent for butternuts, acorns, and beechnuts. I haven't seen such an abundant crop since. Fortunately, my enthusiasm that first year provided me with enough butternuts to last me quite a while. It's a nice feeling to be looking forward to winter again with a store of dry butternuts already stashed away in my back closet.

46

Club Mosses

By November we have already had several hard frosts, and the first snow is just around the corner. Most of summer's green growth has by now turned dry and brittle brown. These weeks between the killing frosts and the first snows are a good time to look at evergreens—and not just evergreen trees. One group of evergreens that are especially interesting are the club mosses.

Club mosses are not mosses. They are more advanced plants, more closely related to ferns. They don't really look like either mosses or ferns, however, so their name and evolutionary connections don't help much in recognizing them. The name *club* may help because it does describe the spore-bearing structures that grow above the small evergreen plants. At this time of year many club mosses sport ripe spore "clubs" that will cover your hands with fine yellow dust if you touch them.

Club mosses look like baby evergreen trees. These small evergreens are already fully grown, however. The fact that club mosses look like baby trees raises a complex question about the evolutionary history of the club mosses that persist today. Why don't they grow bigger? About 300 million years ago, during the period referred to as the Coal Age, club mosses did grow bigger—even bigger than today's trees. The Carboniferous forests that covered much of North America were made up of huge 100-foot tall ferns, horsetails, and club mosses.

When the Carboniferous forests fell and were buried under heavy layers of mud, silt, and sand—eventually to become coal—the giant ferns, horsetails, and club mosses gave way to the smaller versions that we see today. The dimunitive club mosses that look like baby trees can perhaps be described as "babies in reverse." Their ancestors were giants, but growing conditions favored a smaller size. In order to survive, the giants evolved into babies.

Despite their diminished size, club mosses have a life cycle that befits a giant. It takes about seventeen years for them to grow from spore to mature club moss. First, the parent plant has to drop its spores. Spores are not as efficient as seeds. They do not grow up into a mature plant within the next few growing seasons. A spore that finds a suitable environment produces an intermediate plant called a gametophyte. The gametophytes of the club mosses are so small that people rarely notice them. It takes the club moss spore about seven years to produce a fully grown gametophyte.

The gametophyte has both male and female organs on the same plant. The male sperm must find its way to the egg in the female organ in order for the next stage in the club moss's life cycle to begin. If the sperm succeeds in its mission, the egg is fertilized and begins to grow into a recognizable club moss. It may take as long as ten or more years, but eventually the mature spore-producing adult that we can see and identify will appear.

Every club moss you see did not have to start from scratch, however. Club mosses also propagate by growing more roots and longer stems. If you look closely at a community of club mosses and pull gently on a few, you will see that many of them are connected by stems that grow on or just beneath the surface of the ground.

Although these long stems have helped club mosses survive, they have also made some species vulnerable to the attacks of Christmas decorators. Many people pull up the trailing evergreen growths and weave them into Christmas wreaths. A stem pulled up by the roots means the end to over seventeen years' work on the part of the plant. Picking club mosses for Christmas decorations should therefore be discouraged.

Club mosses are one of the simplest of all plant groups to identify because they are quite distinctive, and there are not very many of them in any one area. I've found only five species in my neighborhood. The most abundant is the tree club moss (*Lycopodium obscurum*), which, looking like miniature Christmas trees, grows abundantly in our sugar bush. Another common species, the running pine or Christmas green (*Lycopodium complanatum*), has flatter, more scalelike leaves than the tree club moss.

The shining club moss (*Lycopodium lucidulum*) grows in the damp woods near my brook. This club moss looks more like an evergreen twig than an evergreen tree. It has relatively large, dark green, shiny needles and no spore clubs. The staghorn, or wolf's claw, club moss (*Lycopodium clavatum*) also looks more like tiny twigs than like a tree, but it has smaller, more fringelike needles than the shining club moss. The branching stems look somewhat like deer antlers, and some of them support groups of spore clubs.

A fifth species, ground cedar (*Lycopodium tristachyum*), is not as abundant as the other four. I have noticed only one bed of these miniature "cedars." They look quite a bit like the more common running pine, but they're smaller, more symmetrical, and more firmly anchored in the soil.

Club mosses, or lycopodiums, are small, but because they are evergreens they are easy to notice at this time of year. Their evolutionary history, their long life cycle, and their relative ease of identification make them good subjects for study. Boughton Cobb's *A Field Guide to the Ferns* (Boston: Houghton Mifflin, 1963) will help you identify club mosses. They are described and explained in the back of the book. If you master the club mosses this fall, maybe you'll feel ready to turn to the front of your field guide and address yourself to the club mosses' more numerous cousins, the ferns, next spring.

47

Lichens

If someone sent you on a scavenger hunt and told you to locate a cup for a pixie, food for a reindeer, and a redcoat, you'd probably think the person lived in a fantasy world. But actually all you'd have to do is locate an old fence post or an old pile of wood out in the open someplace, and you'd find all three items in one location.

Pixie cups, reindeer "moss," and British soldiers are all plants called *lichens*—(pronounced *lye-kins*). They are related to the rugged little pioneers that grow on bare rock surfaces and start the incredibly slow process of turning those rocks into soil.

Botanists divide lichens into three classes according to how they grow. Crustose lichens grow like a close-clinging crust; foliose lichens grow in leafier, more papery arrangements; and fruticose lichens grow in little stalks or branches. All three of the "fantasy" lichens are fruticose, and they all belong to the same genus—*Cladonia*. They grow in delicate little beds intermixed with one another and sometimes with mosses and club mosses. Theirs is a miniature but beautiful world that Vermont author John Bland labeled the "Forests of Lilliput."

The pixie cup looks just the way its common name would suggest. A small, gray-green goblet less than half an inch tall, it has a capacity of perhaps one drop of dew. Where you find one pixie cup, you'll probably find several, some for bigger "pixies," and some for "pixies" far too young to be drinking out of goblets. The "pixies" who left them must have had a most decorous and orderly party because all the goblets stand upright.

Reindeer moss is a white-green branching lichen. When I first saw it, I thought that it must be named after a reindeer's antlers because it looked so much like what I imagined a reindeer's antlers to look like. But I found out later that the reason it's called reindeer moss is that reindeer feed on it. The reindeer moss that grows near where I live also grows in the Arctic, and reindeer and caribou spend their summers grazing in pastures of these brittle lichens.

The British soldiers stand out from the other lichens because of their red tops. Most lichens are a parched green in color, varying from an almost white-green to a split-pea-soup-green if the lichen is full of moisture. The British soldier has a tiny red cap at the top of a light green stalk. These "soldiers" stand among the pixies' "goblets" and the reindeer's "moss" in apparent disarray. You'd think that their red caps would make them vulnerable to an enemy attack, but they occupy an unmilitary world. They're probably safe just as they are, brightly colored and scattered comfortably out of formation.

Lichens are unusual plants. They are fascinating to look at even if you're not interested in their physiology. With a magnifying glass you could spend hours looking at them and theorizing about what they are, what they do, and how they got there.

From a scientific point of view they are even more fascinating. A lichen is not really a plant in the same sense that a wild flower or a tree is. A lichen is actually two separate plants living in close cooperation with one another. One is a fungus, and the other is an alga.

The shape of the lichen is determined by the fungus. The

job of the fungus is to provide protection, stability, moisture, and minerals. Because it has no chlorophyll, it cannot produce food. Conveniently, the alga is a green plant and can manufacture food for both partners. And the alga's chlorophyll gives the lichen its greenish tinge.

This cooperative interdependence between two living organisms is called symbiosis. A lichen is actually a symbiosis of two plants rather than an individual plant in its own right. The word *lichen,* however, is used to refer to this two-in-one plant as if it were a single plant. To call every lichen a *fungus-alga* would be too cumbersome.

Lichens can grow in more severe circumstances than any other plant. They are also among the slowest growing and longest-lived plants known to botanists. But, ironically, these slow-growing, long-lived, rugged little pioneers are extremely sensitive to air pollution. A survey conducted in Montreal showed that lichen populations give a clear indication of air quality. No lichens grew where there was too much sulfur dioxide in the air. So here we are with a plant that can endure amazing extremes of heat and cold, rain and drought, and exposure to unbroken winds, yet it will perish in the air we have created in our cities.

Polluted air, of course, affects other plants, too, but lichens are especially sensitive because of their relationship to water. Most plants absorb water through their roots, so the water has been filtered through the soil. Lichens don't have roots and don't grow in soil; they absorb their water directly from rain or dew. Whatever atmospheric pollutants are dissolved in the rain or dew find their way directly into the lichen. The fruticose lichens, such as pixie cups, reindeer moss, and British soldiers, are the most sensitive to polluted air. Some species of foliose lichens have a greater tolerance, and the crustose lichens are the most tolerant of all.

After I read about the lichen counts in Montreal, I raced around to some of my favorite places to look for lichens, and I'm glad to report abundant populations everywhere. Some look like small maps growing on rocks and old stone walls. Almost every tree in the sugar bush has patches of light-green foliose lichens, and of course my fantasy lichens were right where I left them, growing profusely on the old loading ramp left behind when the logging stopped.

I hope the day will never come when the air in my neighborhood threatens lichens. An excess of sulfur dioxide would ruin more than just my scavenger hunts.

48

Birds' Nests

Late fall, after the leaves have dropped but before the heavy snows have begun to fall, is a good time to study birds' nests. The nests, of course, are empty, but they're well worth looking for if you're interested in knowing who your bird neighbors were last summer and probably will be again next spring. Birds don't return to the same nests, but certain species prefer certain habitats. If you identify an abandoned nest in the fall, it's likely that the same species—if not the same individual—will raise a family in the vicinity next spring.

When I say "study" birds' nests, I don't mean collecting and dissecting them. That would be illegal. I mean looking for nests around your house or wherever you take your walks, identifying them if you can, and remembering that you saw a nest of that species in that habitat. When spring comes you can listen for bird songs, and, if you've done your homework on nests in the fall, you won't be tempted to disturb bird nurseries in order to see what kind of nest the singer is defending.

The nests most obvious at this time of year are those in the upper branches of roadside trees. It takes a pair of binoculars to see the details of these nests, but, because only certain species nest in tall trees close to roads, identification should not be difficult.

The robin, for instance, is a roadside nester. I have a robin's nest in one of the large maples that line the road in front of my house. Another maple holds a blue jay's nest. Although blue jays generally prefer conifers, they sometimes nest in deciduous trees. Both robins and blue jays are accustomed to human beings and don't seem to mind nesting close to our roads and houses.

I heard and saw the robins last spring, but I can't say that I noticed the blue jay family. Blue jays are surprisingly quiet around their nests. The nest the robins left is a substantial-looking structure made of grasses, weed stalks, and other odds and ends held together by mud. The blue jay's nest is a bigger, looser, twiggier affair. Its outer twigs look as if they're about to come apart.

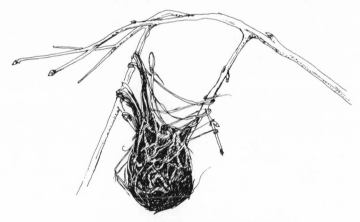

NORTHERN ORIOLE NEST

Two other birds that sometimes nest in roadside trees are the northern oriole and the scarlet tanager. The oriole's nest is a pouch rather than a cup, and it's woven strongly enough to support the weight of the female and her eggs as they hang suspended from the end of a branch often as high as sixty feet above the ground.

The scarlet tanager likes to build its nest high in an oak tree. The nest is loosely constructed of twigs and rootlets. It looks small and flimsy. If I were a bird and were going to lay my eggs up as high as the scarlet tanager sometimes does, I think I'd want a more substantial nest. But I suppose they know what they're doing.

Moving away from houses and roadsides and into the edges of open woods, you will begin finding medium-high, maybe even eye-level, nests. The wood thrush, the rose-breasted grosbeak, and the red-eyed vireo all nest at about ten feet above the ground. Wood thrushes build compact nests held together with mud, but they include loose bark, paper, and leaves in their construction. These materials have a way of dangling from the nests, making the nests look a little bedraggled at this time of year.

The rose-breasted grosbeak's construction techniques are as casual as the scarlet tanager's, but because the nest isn't as high it doesn't seem quite as precarious. The nest I saw was a loose assortment of twigs with the sky quite visible through it as I looked up from below.

The nest of the red-eyed vireo is a delicate little structure that hangs suspended from a forked branch. It's held together and attached to the branch by spider webbing. The two red-eyed vireo nests I've seen in trees nearby were too high for me to study closely. I'm still looking for one at eye level so that I can see how the spider webbing works. With all the red-eyed vireos I hear singing in my neighborhood during the nesting season, I'm hopeful of finding just the nest I'm looking for.

Other nests less easy to find but equally interesting are the ground nests of the hermit thrush, the veery, and the oven-bird. They are always well camouflaged. You might have to stumble upon an occupied nest next spring to locate one of them, but I know they're out there because I've heard each of these birds singing in my neighborhood.

Bluebirds, chickadees, nuthatches, and woodpeckers are cavity nesters, so you'll have to go poking into holes to locate their nests. In the case of bluebirds, you can set out a bluebird house and watch them come and go during their nesting season. When they leave at the end of the season, you can open the house and look at the nest they built inside.

Studying nests in fall and winter and bird songs in spring will help you identify your bird neighbors without disturbing them. Much of learning about wild animals involves speculating about what's happening without witnessing it. Personally, I prefer to honor the birds' privacy during the nesting season. I can learn everything I want to know about their nests in the fall when I'm not disturbing the nest builders and their families.

49

Goldfinches

The first visitor to my bird feeder this year was a male goldfinch. It didn't take him long to spread the word. Shortly after I first noticed him, two other goldfinches arrived to feast on the fresh supply of sunflower seeds I had just put out.

When people think of goldfinches, they picture bright yellow birds. The birds at my feeder had enough yellow left on them that I could identify them as males, but the brilliant summer plumage had given way to winter drab. I was glad to have a chance to look closely at the winter coloring while the birds fed right outside my kitchen window.

Many birds change their feathers for winter. After they have finished nesting, they experience what is called a postnuptial molt. The males lose their distinctive courtship coloring and take on the more neutral colors of the females and the young. In the case of the wood duck this postnuptial plumage, appropriately called an eclipse, lasts only a month or so. The regal male has his courtship plumage back by the end of the summer, and he flies south for the winter in his wedding attire. The goldfinch, on the other hand, stays drab throughout the winter. He will molt again in the spring—his prenuptial molt—to prepare him for his duties as suitor, husband, and father.

All this changing of plumage would seem like waste and vanity if courtship were its only function. But molting is important for another reason, too. A bird's life is not easy on feathers, and the molt is its way of changing into new feathers on a regular basis.

Different birds molt in different ways. Some birds, like the penguin, shed all their feathers at once. The new feathers, which grow simultaneously all over the penguin's body, push away the old feathers. Ducks and geese molt gradually, but they lose all their flight feathers at once and are temporarily grounded while they're waiting for their new flight feathers to grow back.

The goldfinch is typical of perching birds in that its molt is gradual and symmetrical. It sheds a few feathers at a time and is already growing some new ones back as the old ones fall away. The flight feathers go in pairs, one from each side at a time, and therefore the goldfinch is never flightless.

Female goldfinches molt, too, but because they stay olive drab the new feathers are not as noticeable. The young goldfinch goes through several sets of feathers in its first year. Born naked, the hatchling first grows down feathers. The down is shortly replaced by drab but functional contour and flight feathers. For most of its first year the young goldfinch is attired in these nondescript feathers called the juvenal plumage. The full adult coloring won't come until the prenuptial molt the next spring.

Males, females, and young look very much alike during the winter except for subtle markings noticeable only from close up—such as when they're at a window feeder. The male retains patches of yellow on his throat and shoulders. Although he loses his black cap, his wings and tail stay dark black. The female is olive without the yellow patches that distinguish the male. Her wings are dark brown rather than jet black. The immature goldfinch is as drab as the female, but if it's a male he already has his jet black wings.

Goldfinches build their nests and raise their young late in

the season. While other birds are working overtime feeding their hungry young and sometimes even raising a second brood, goldfinches are still flying around feeding themselves, singing, and, in general, enjoying the summer. When thistles go to seed in July and August, it's time for the goldfinches to build their nests. They use thistle down to line their nests, and thistle seeds are a favorite food.

THISTLE

The female is the family architect. She usually builds her nest in an upright fork in a small tree near an abundant supply of thistles. The nest is small and tight. Because goldfinch nests are tight enough to hold water, the young sometimes drown during heavy rains.

The female also does all the incubating, and she is conscientious in her duties. The male brings her food—partially digested, regurgitated weed seeds—and sings to her while she's sitting on the nest. When the young hatch the male feeds both the female and the young—which keeps him busy for a few weeks. It takes the eggs about twelve to fourteen days to hatch, and it takes another eleven to fifteen days for the young to leave the nest. The female begins to feed herself and help feed the young toward the end of this stint, but occasionally she will still beg for food as she did when she was brooding. The male ignores her regression, and I can't blame him.

Goldfinch mates are attentive to one another, and they are good parents to their young. They are not very good housekeepers, however. Most birds remove their youngs' excrement as soon as it appears—usually shortly after they've been fed. Goldfinches sometimes do and sometimes don't, and the result is a messy nest by the end of the season. One way to identify a goldfinch's nest is by the rim of caked excrement.

Goldfinches are very sociable birds except for the brief period when they are nesting and raising their young. They travel in flocks and seem to enjoy each other's company. The three goldfinches that have spent time at my feeder do not seem at all competitive. They don't mind the close quarters of the feeder, and they seem to enjoy sharing the wealth.

Watching birds at a feeder is one of many ways to enjoy winter. The drab but happy little goldfinches that seem to take such pleasure in the sunflower seeds I have put out for them give me pleasure in return. Even if their bright summer plumage is gone for now, these lively little birds make me think of summer sunshine.

50

Birches

Vermont's most famous trees are the maples. They give us syrup in the spring and colorful foliage in the fall. Summer and winter, however, the birches have their sway. Summer visitors leave with memories of white birch trees growing along rivers, brooks, lakeshores, and roadsides. Winter visitors can't help but notice the white against white that accents the stark beauty of our winter landscapes.

Although the white, or paper, birch is probably the best known of our birches, they come in other colors, too: gray, yellow, and black. Each birch has its own characteristics and makes it own contributions to the natural world. Each, therefore, deserves some separate recognition and credit.

But first let's consider their similarities. All birches have shallow, fibrous root systems like those of elms and beeches rather than taproots like oaks and hickories. Birch roots grow horizontally, branching, rebranching, and spreading in a thick mat throughout the soil.

All birches also shed their leaves for the winter. The dying leaves contribute rich golds and yellows to our fall foilage. Birch leaves, buds, and twigs are arranged alternately on their branches rather than opposite each other like the maple's. Winter is the best time to look closely at the buds, twigs, and branches and the basic shape of the leafless tree.

Although the colors and textures of the bark of the four birch trees are different, all four have pronounced horizontal marks on the bark called lenticels. The lenticels, which look like dash marks, help the tree breathe.

Finally, all the birches reproduce by means of structures called catkins. Both male and female catkins occur on the same tree. The male catkins hang from the twigs. They are formed during the growing season and wait out the winter in tight, hard little clusters. Early in the spring they lengthen and shed pollen that floats to the female catkins. Pollination occurs before the leaves appear. During spring and summer the fertilized female catkin grows into a fruit that looks like a little pine cone. Composed of winged seeds, these cones stay on the trees throughout the winter and provide food for birds and other hungry animals.

Among the birches the white birch is the most familiar because its smooth, chalky, peeling bark attracts the attention of even those who have no special interest in trees. The chalky texture of the bark invites people to touch it, and the peeling of the sheets tempts people to pull off the bark. Touching the bark is an excellent way to learn about it, but peeling it off leaves ugly scars.

It's easy to confuse gray birch with white birch. Gray birch bark is white, too, but it doesn't peel as the white birch's does. Also, each branch has a dark Fu Manchu mustache where it joins the tree trunk. Whereas white birches grow singly, gray birches frequently appear in clumps, growing as a group from the roots of a predecessor.

Gray birches are called "pioneers" because they are among the first trees to grow in an abandoned field or an area that has been cut over or burned. But gray birches don't live very long. They are "intolerant," which means they do not compete well once other trees have begun to grow nearby and create shade. White birches live longer and can be seen among other hardwoods or sometimes in pure stands in a young forest.

Once a gray birch dies, it rots faster than most other trees. Hard, cup-shaped fungi grow on the trunk while it's still standing. Within a short time the tree is so weak that you can push it over with little trouble. Once it's on the ground, the wood decomposes rapidly and mixes into the soil. The bark usually outlasts the wood and can be found lying around with no wood left inside it.

At the other extreme from the small, short-lived gray birch is the large, long-lived yellow birch. Whereas gray birches are pioneers, yellow birches live to be members of a mature forest. In appearance yellow birch looks somewhat like white birch, but it has shiny golden-yellow bark. The bark peels differently, too, separating in thin little curls rather than in the sheets and strips more typical of the white birch.

My favorite yellow birches grow among huge hemlocks in a swamp near where I live. These particular yellow birches began growing on old logs or stumps and grew strong roots around these temporary supports. The logs and stumps have long since rotted away, and now the yellow birches look as if they're standing on stilts—or maybe on tiptoes—to avoid the wetness of the swamp.

Yellow birch twigs have a slight wintergreen taste that deer seem to appreciate, for deer browse the twigs of yellow birch more heavily than the twigs of the less tasty white and gray birches. The bark itself is a favorite of porcupines, snowshoe hares, cottontail rabbits, and beavers.

The black, or sweet, birch is the least abundant birch tree in my area. In fact, I've seen only one since I've known what I was looking for, and it was growing in a most unlikely spot—out of a rockslide at the foot of a steep cliff. It was a rugged and sizable tree. I was amazed at its tenacity, growing there among the rocks. I wouldn't have known it was a black birch if a friend hadn't invited me to chew on a twig. Black birch has a strong taste of wintergreen. Birch beer, a sweet and delicious soft drink, is made from the sap of black birch.

Robert Frost did a good job of celebrating birches in his famous poem entitled "Birches." Although he was probably thinking about the small and flexible gray birches in the line, "One could do worse than be a swinger of birches," his title pays tribute to all our birches.

51

Nuthatches

With so many insects to be eaten to keep the natural world in balance, it's only logical that there should be birds looking for them from every possible angle. Brown creepers start at the bottom of a tree and find insects hidden in bark crevices as they spiral upward around the tree trunk. Woodpeckers land on a tree trunk and jump upward or downward in their search for insects. They also dig into the tree to expose woodboring larvae. Chickadees dance acrobatically around the twigs, searching for insect eggs and larvae. The job that remains for the nuthatches is to climb down the tree trunk head first, eating whatever insects they can discover from that angle.

It takes a special kind of body to be an upside-down bird. Nuthatches have short legs, strong feet, and a broad flat tail. When they are climbing down a tree, one foot is sometimes turned completely around with the toes headed up the tree. The other foot is pointed downward, in the same direction as the body. The leg that is reversed is stretched back beside the tail. The other leg is under the breast. Like most other perching birds, nuthatches have three toes forward and one back, but the nuthatch's back toe has an especially long claw. These legs, feet, and claws are uniquely adapted for walking down a tree trunk. Nuthatches do this as easily as most other birds might perch on a limb or hop along the ground.

Brown creepers and woodpeckers use their tails for extra support when they're clinging to a tree trunk. The nuthatch never braces its tail against the tree. The tail, in fact, seems designed to be out of the way. It's short and flat, looking as if someone might have snipped it off neatly with a pair of scissors. In a characteristic pose, a nuthatch clings close to the tree trunk, head downward, its feet the only support, and its beak pointed directly away from the tree. In this position it seems to communicate that upside down is the most comfortable way to view the world.

For all their special adaptations, nuthatches don't spend all their time climbing head-first down tree trunks. In winter they like nuts and seeds better than they like insects. White-breasted nuthatches, who are inhabitants of deciduous woods, are very fond of acorns. Although they are called nuthatches, their long slender beaks do not look like the nut-crackers they'd need to break into an acorn shell. Nuthatches cleverly wedge an acorn into a crevice and peck at it until the shell breaks. Red-breasted nuthatches prefer a different habitat and different seeds. They live in coniferous woods and eat the seeds they find in cones. Pine seeds are a favorite. These smaller nuthatches use their beaks to pry open the scales of a cone and to eat the seeds they find there.

Both types of nuthatches can be seen in winter. The white-breasted nuthatch comes to feeders quite regularly. Often it chases chickadees away and grabs a sunflower seed for itself. It carries the seed off to a crevice where it either stores it for later use or pecks it open to eat right away. The red-breasted nuthatch will come to a feeder only if the feeder is located close enough to the cover of coniferous trees.

Both nuthatches are attractive birds, but to my eyes the red-breasted is prettier. The white-breasted nuthatch looks bold and aggressive with its black eyes staring out of solid white cheeks. The red-breasted nuthatch has a black line through its eye and a white eyebrow above the line. It also has a rust-colored breast. Its coloring is more appealing to me than the stark blacks, whites, and grays of its larger relative.

I'm always fascinated when I see either of the nuthatches coming down a tree. They seem so perfectly at ease in their upside down progress. With all their adaptations, they are, of course, at ease. From their point of view, if they even notice me looking up at them, I'm the one who's upside down.

52

The Big Dipper

On a clear, cold winter night everything seems motionless; it seems as if the whole universe is frozen. The stars are pinpoints of freezing light. The moon is an icy mirror, reflecting cold air back at me. As I walk down the road—briskly to stay warm—I feel as if I am the only motion anywhere. It is an illusion, of course; my short walk does not even register among the larger movements of the earth and stars. The Big Dipper is the key.

When the stars first appear on a winter evening, the Big Dipper looks as if it's standing on its handle. As the night goes on, this familiar group of stars moves in a huge, counterclockwise circle, emptying its contents in the middle of the night, then starting back down to scoop up another serving. At dawn, when it's halfway around the circle, it fades and finishes the circle during daylight hours when we can't see it. By the next evening it will be standing on its handle again.

If I walk down the road two or three times between sunset and midnight, I can watch the Big Dipper's progress. But the Big Dipper's apparent progress actually records my own. It's the earth beneath my feet that's moving, rotating on its axis once every twenty-four hours. It's because the earth and I are rotating that the Big Dipper appears to be circling in the sky.

Because the earth and I are also orbiting around the sun, the Big Dipper seems to be in a slightly different position in its circle if I look at it at exactly the same time every night. It is about four minutes ahead of where it was the night before. As the months and seasons pass, the four-minute differences add up. On a winter evening at nine o'clock the Big Dipper is standing on its handle. On a spring evening at nine it is high in the sky emptying its contents. On a summer evening at nine it has its handle up and its dipper down. On a fall evening at nine it is low in the sky with the dipper in a position to be holding liquid again.

To locate the center of the circle the Big Dipper seems to make, imagine a straight line through the stars at the front end of the dipper and follow it until you see a bright star. That star is the North Star, also called Polaris and Pole Star. The North Pole of the earth points toward this star. Therefore, as the earth rotates on its axis, the North Star seems stationary, and the stars closest to it seem to move in a circle around it. Extending from the North Star is another dipper—the Little Dipper—which is more difficult to see than the Big Dipper. Night sailors and other star watchers are so familiar with the positions these two Dippers assume throughout the night that they can read them like a clock. Just as the arms of a clock are set to record the earth's rotation as they sweep around in their measured circle, the apparent motion of the two Dippers records—counterclockwise —how much we have turned.

Watching the two Dippers helps me conceptualize the earth's motion even if I can't feel it, and conceptualizing the earth's motion makes me, for all my walking, feel relatively still. But just when I think I have the problem of motion in proper perspective, I remember that our whole solar system is hurtling through space at the rate of millions of miles per day. And the stars, which are outside our solar system, are moving, too, all at unimaginable speeds. At that point I have to quit looking at the Dippers and start walking again to remind myself that for all practical purposes the earth and stars are standing still. I have to move my own slow self back up the road if I want to keep from freezing.

Epilogue

When I first started writing the essays that became this book, I was leading school children on nature walks four or five times a week. I didn't find much time to take the kind of nature walk I would like to recommend. With children in tow, two things are happening to keep you from experiencing the full benefit of a walk.

One problem is noise. I am not being critical of children. I would be alarmed if a child made no sounds for an extended period of time. But noise, of course, alerts wildlife to human presence. So if you have children with you, the animals that you might have seen will probably be long gone by the time you approach where they were.

The second problem with a walk with children is questions. Children ask many challenging questions. But if they keep asking you "What's this?", "What's that?", and "Why?", you are going to be so busy answering (or trying to answer) their questions that you will not have the time or inclination to ask your own. Silence and curiosity are the two most important things you can take with you on a nature walk.

Guiding children is a satisfying experience, but I also cherish the walks I take alone. I like to move slowly and quietly, looking at things, sitting still for a while, maybe taking notes on something unusual. When I take one of these refreshing walks, I ask much more than I answer. It's these open-ended questions that keep me returning to the woods and fields and banks of a river to ask again.

I like to take plenty of time when I go walking alone. Moving slowly enables you to see, hear, and smell more of your surroundings. If your attention is on where you are rather than where you are trying to get, you are going to notice more. Moving slowly also keeps your noise to a minimum. Silence is the key to seeing wildlife. Sitting still is even better than walking if you want to see animals in action. If you can be quiet for long enough, animals will forget you're there and resume whatever activity you might have interrupted when you first arrived.

When I take my solitary walks, I tend to have attention problems. I have the bad habit of letting my attention wander inward to thoughts that are invited by my being alone in the woods. If I don't prompt myself, I fall deep into a reverie that distracts my attention from what is right in front of me. One technique I use to keep my attention focused outward is to touch things—the bark of a tree, a fungus growing on a rotting log, a patch of moss, leaves, or flowers. In touching I notice details that I might not have seen from a distance. I try to concentrate on details that distinguish what I'm looking at from other similar things.

I don't carry field guides with me on my solitary nature walks unless I intend to concentrate on a special subject like wild flowers, ferns, or animal tracks. Observing and remembering details is what will help me identify whatever it is I've examined when I get home. In my opinion, developing an ability to observe closely and remember distinguishing details is more useful to a beginning naturalist than learning the names of things the first time you see them.

Even if I have found myself having to return to a certain spot, field book in hand, to identify a plant I thought I had looked at closely enough to remember, I think the process is worth it. I may be doing twice the work with this method, but I'm afraid I wouldn't pay as much attention to details and to my own observations if I had a field guide along the first time.

The best aspect of solitary nature walks is the surprises. When I'm with children or with another person, somehow these surprises seem not to happen. One surprise I still remember is seeing a ruffed grouse for the first time. It was a female with her young. I think I was more startled than she was. When my heart slowed down again I found myself fascinated by her actions. She staggered around not far from me, dragging a wing as if she were injured. Of course, I felt sorry for her all the way home. But when I described the incident to a friend, he explained that she was pretending. She was putting on her "broken wing act" to keep my attention on her while her young ones scurried into the underbrush.

Another surprise that still excites me even though it's happened more than once is the crash of underbrush as a white-tailed deer takes off. The leaps and bounces and the white flag disappearing into the woods draw my eyes after the deer. Seeing a deer always makes me feel privileged—as if I have visited a world much wilder than the well-traveled trails on which I have guided.

A nature walk can be an educational tool, as it is when I lead school children. Or it can be a social or recreational experience, as it is when a group of friends decide to hike to a new or familiar spot together. The kind of nature walk I am recommending, however, is a very private and personal experience. I return from such walks refreshed and excited again about how much there is to learn. It's on these solitary walks that all the facts and field guide information suddenly connect. And I feel myself reaching a new stage of awareness in my effort to learn about nature.

Resources for the Beginning Naturalist

BOOKS

There is a wealth of written material available to help you answer your questions. Become a browser in bookstores and libraries. Look at books that other people use—especially the ones with well-worn covers. A nature center library or gift shop is a goldmine.

I own three books that I refer to on almost every subject I become curious about. Anna Botsford Comstock's *Handbook of Nature Study* (Ithaca: Comstock Publishing Company, 1911) is a classic. No one has yet produced as wise and comprehensive an introduction to the natural world. *Fieldbook of Natural History* by Laurence Palmer, revised by Seymour Fowler (New York: McGraw-Hill, 1975) is an excellent reference book. They say a little bit about almost everything from astronomy to mammals. A third book tells me who eats what, which is the key to understanding interactions in the natural world. I am a little uncomfortable with the mathematical exactness of its statistics, but I use it as a guide. The book is entitled *American Wildlife and Plants: A Guide to Wildlife Food Habits.* It's by Alexander Martin, Herbert Zim, and Arnold Nelson (New York: Dover, 1961).

As you become interested in different subjects, you might want to buy field guides to help you identify what you see. Several publishing companies have field guide series. Houghton Mifflin, for instance, publishes the Peterson Series, which includes field guides for about twenty different subjects. Putnam also has a series of about twenty volumes called Nature Field Books. Golden Press publishes several field guides—not to be confused with their small, introductory Golden Guides. The Golden Field Guides are booksize and booklength. So far there are five: birds, rocks and minerals, seashells, trees, and amphibians. Finally, Doubleday publishes three bird books, an insect guide, and a wildflower guide. I prefer different series for different subjects.

For birds, I prefer the Golden Field Guide to *Birds of North America* by Chandler Robbins, Bertel Bruun, and Herbert Zim (New York: Golden Press, 1966). All the information you need for identification is together on facing pages. The Peterson Series guide by Roger Tory Peterson (Boston: Houghton Mifflin, 1934) is also standard, but I find it more difficult to use. The National Audubon Society has recently published a new field guide that includes photographs (New York: Alfred A. Knopf, 1977).

For trees, I prefer the Golden Field Guide to *Trees of North America* by Frank Brockman (New York: Golden Press, 1968). The colored illustrations and range maps are helpful. For wildflowers, I have become attached to a new book that doesn't belong to a series. It is so easy to use that even elementary school children have mastered the key. Look for *Newcomb's Wildflower Guide* by Lawrence Newcomb (Boston: Little Brown, 1977). For ferns and club mosses, I use the Peterson Series field guide by Boughton Cobb (Boston: Houghton Mifflin, 1963).

For mammals, I use two Peterson Series field guides, one to mammals by William Burt and Richard Grossenheider and one to tracks by Olaus Murie (Boston: Houghton Mifflin, 1952 and 1954).

In addition to my reference books and field guides I have one slender paperback that has helped me integrate what I am learning: John Storer's *Web of Life* (New York: Signet, 1953). I re-read it periodically to remind myself that everything connects.

MAGAZINES, PAMPHLETS, AND ORGANIZATIONS

My favorite magazines are *Natural History* (American Museum of Natural History), *National Wildlife* (National Wildlife Federation), and the *Conservationist* (New York Department of Environmental Conservation). I also read two children's magazines: *Ranger Rick* (National Wildlife Federation) and *The Curious Naturalist* (Massachusetts Audubon Society). I leaf through *Audubon, National Geographic,* and *Smithsonian* each month and read an occasional article that interests me.

I belong to the Massachusetts Audubon Society, which sends its members a newsletter ten times a year and a very handsome yearbook. They also offer numerous educational pamphlets at reasonable prices. Cornell University also publishes an inexpensive series of leaflets I've found helpful. They're called Cornell Science Leaflets. Finally, I belong to a Vermont organization called the Vermont Institute of Natural Science. Their newsletters and annual natural history magazine provide me with information specific to Vermont.

BINOCULARS

Optics are complicated. If you haven't had much experience with binoculars, you can wind up paying a lot of money for a pair of binoculars that might not be suited to your needs. I recommend writing to Mirakel Optical Company, 331 Mansion Street, West Coxsackie, New York 12192. Tell them what you plan to use your binoculars for and what you'd like to pay. They will recommend the best binoculars for your needs at your price. They also service the binoculars they sell.

HAND LENSES

Don't buy a reading glass by mistake. A reading glass is a large magnifying glass of the type Sherlock Holmes always seemed to have with him. It gives only three power magnification, so it will not help you see flower parts, insect eyes, and other such things. I own a small, ten power hand lens that I bought at a university bookstore for about $5.00. The glass is about ¾ inch in diameter and it folds back into a protective metal case. I wear my hand lens on a piece of string around my neck—like an oversized senior ring.

PEOPLE

People are your best resources. Find individuals who seem to know something about the natural world and ask them questions. Attend lectures, take short courses and workshops, or participate in activities at a nature center.

As you encounter naturalists, make distinctions. Seek out and cherish the company of people whose way of knowing— and sharing—encourages you to learn more.

INDEX

Accipiters, 144-49
Acorns, 9, 69, 161, 171, 193
Adaptations, 37, 66, 77, 80, 122, 126, 194. *See also* Survival (of species)
Air pollution, 178-79
Algae, 87, 178
Amphibians, 3, 14, 60, 91, 98, 144
Animals, homes for, 21, 23-24, 35-36 *(See also* Burrows; Dens; Tunnels, animal); identifying, 8-10, 25-27, 53-54, 139-40, 157-59, 160-62, 163-65, 199. *See also* names of individual animals
Annelids, 131
Annuals, 127
Antennae, insect, 114-15
Ants, 12-13, 113-16
Aphids, 115
Apple Trees, 78, 80, 164
Audubon Society, 7, 45

"Baby bird crisis," 81-85
Bacteria, 87, 89, 120
Badgers, 25, 26
Bark: as food for animals, 9, 24, 30-31, 34, 36, 164; as home for insects, 12, 19, 79, 112, 136, 143, 192; birch, 189-90
Bats, 8, 30, 95, 157-58
Bears, 8, 14, 30, 35, 162
Beavers, 34-37, 159, 190
Bees, 11, 47-48, 110-12, 113, 144
Beetles, 133, 154

Bentley, "Snowflake," 22-23
Berries, 117-19
Biennials, 76, 123, 127
Big Dipper, 195-97
Binoculars, 5, 85, 149, 180, 203-204
Bioluminescence, 104-106
Birch trees, 31, 36, 164, 188-91
Bird feeders, 3-6, 44-45, 184, 187, 193
Birds, 81-85, 119, 144-49, 157-59, 192-94; identifying, vii, 3-7, 12, 18-21, 44-46, 67-70, 180-83; nests of, 21, 65-66, 81, 85, 180-83, 185-86; songs of, 71-73, 180, 183. *See also* Migration, bird; names of individual birds
Black-eyed Susans, 107
Bland, John, 176
Blue jays, 3, 181
Bluebirds, 21, 183
Bobcats, 9, 33, 35, 162, 164
British soldiers (plant), 176, 177
Buds, 3, 15-17, 48-49, 109, 120, 188; as food for birds and animals, 6, 164
Bumblebees, 110, 112. *See also* Bees
Burrows, 8, 25, 27-28, 29, 153-54, 160-61. *See also* Dens; Tunnels, animal
Buteos, 145-49
Buttercups, 107-109
Butterflies, 11, 97
Butternuts, 169-71
Buzzards, 145

206

Carboniferous period, 100, 172-73
Carnivores, 25-26, 162
Carpenter ants, 12
Carrots, 123-24
Caterpillars, 12, 66, 78-80, 83, 110, 166-68
Catkins, 189
Cats, domestic, 9, 31, 46, 81-82, 158, 162, 164
Cattails, 127-30
Centipedes, 135-37, 154
Chameleons, 90-92
Cherry trees, 78-80
Chickadees, 5, 6-7, 12, 183, 192, 193
Chickens, 146-48
Chipmunks, 8, 14, 27, 30, 133, 160-62
Chlorophyll, 178
Classification (of animals and plants), 26, 92
Climax (vegetation), 87
Clitellum, 153, 156
Club mosses, 172-75, 176
Cluster flies, 14
Cocoons, 12, 79-80, 156, 167
Colonies, insect, 11, 79-80, 110-16
Cottony cushion scales, 141
Courtship, 67, 69, 71-73, 104, 184. *See also* Mating
Coyotes, 9, 33, 35, 162, 164
Crows, 7
Cuckoos, 79-80

Daisies, 107
Damselflies, 95, 100
Dandelions, 74-77, 107
Darwin, Charles, 155
Deer, 9, 24, 30, 81, 159, 190, 200
Deer mice, 9, 21, 30, 159
Dens, 53-55. *See also* Burrows; Tunnels, animal
Diapause, 3, 11, 23
Division of labor, in insects, 113-16
Dogs, 9, 32, 54, 81-82, 164
Down (feathers), 185
Downy woodpeckers, 5, 12, 18-21
Dragonflies, 95, 97-100
Ducks, 37, 67-70, 184, 185

Earthworms, 66, 83, 87, 105, 131-32, 136, 153-56
Echolocation, 157-58
Eclipse (plumage), 68, 184
Ecology, 37, 134. *See also* Adaptations; Survival (of species)

Edible wild foods, 56-59
Efts, 90-92
Eggs: bird, 181, 186-87; insect, 78, 93, 95, 97-98, 105, 112, 113-14, 120-21, 133, 142, 155-56, 167. *See also* Life cycles
Endangered species, 69
Equinox, 42, 47
Erosion, 86, 89
Evening grosbeaks, 5
Evergreens, 30-31, 164, 172-75, 181, 193
Eyes, animal, 157-58

Fall: animals in the, 33, 160-61; birds in the, 68, 180, 183; insects in the, 78, 80, 111, 143, 167-68; plants in the, 74, 130, 172, 174-75, 188
False hellebore, 57-59
Feathers, bird, 72, 81, 158, 184-85
Ferns, 172, 173, 175
Field guides, 5, 7, 10, 83, 175, 199, 201-203
Field mice, 30, 133. *See also* Mice
Fielde, Adele, 115
Fireflies, 103-106
Fish, 14
Fishers, 9, 33, 162, 164
Fleas, 13-14
Florets, 77, 125
Flowers, vii, 76, 107-109, 117, 120, 123-25, 127-30
Flycatchers, 21
Flying squirrels, 21, 159
Food chains, 9-10, 14, 37
Forest floor, 23, 47, 90, 140, 160, 170
"Forests of Lilliput," 176
Fossils, 100, 140
Foxes, 14, 33, 53-55; as predators, 9, 28, 33, 162, 164
Frogs, 60-64, 70, 91, 98, 133, 154
Frost, Robert, 191
Fruit trees, 78-80
Fruits, 117-19
Fungi, 87, 115, 120, 177-78, 190

Galls, 120-22
Game birds, as food for hawks, 144-49
Gametophytes, 173
Garden, 153-56
Gastropods, 132
Geese, 185

Glowworms, 103
Goldenrod, 120-22
Goldfinches, 184-87
Gophers, 25, 26-27
Green Mountain Audubon Nature
  Center, vii
Groundhog Day, 25, 29
Groundhogs, 25-29. *See also*
  Woodchucks
Gulls, 7

Hairy woodpeckers, 5, 12, 18-21
Hand lens, 22, 76, 107, 204
Hares, 9, 30, 163-65, 190. *See also*
  Rabbits
Harrier, 149
Harvard Forest, 43
Hawks, 46, 140, 144-49, 157, 162,
  164
Hedgehogs, 25-26
Hellebore, 59
"Hemlock," 57, 124
Hermit thrushes, 182
Hibernation, 3, 64, 92, 143, 161
Hibernators, animal, 8, 23-24, 25-29.
  See also Winter, animals in the
Hives, insect, 11, 110-12
Honey, 11, 110, 112
Honeybees, 11, 110, 112. *See also*
  Bees
Hornets, 11, 110-12
Host plants, 120-22
Houseflies, 11

Indians, 43, 57
Insects: as food for animals, 13-14,
  24, 63-64, 88, 136-37, 139-40, 157;
  as food for birds, 12, 20-21, 46,
  66, 83, 144-49; as food for other
  insects, 38-39, 41, 98, 112, 142;
  food for, 37, 78-80, 98, 110, 112,
  120-22; identifying, 3, 11-14,
  78-80, 93, 97-102, 103-106;
  pollination by, 109, 112, 125-26.
  See also Life cycles, insect; names
  of individual insects
Isabella tiger moths, 167

Jumping mice, 8, 30
Juncos, 5

Ladybugs, 11, 141-43
Larvae, insect, 11, 78, 95, 97,
  113-14, 120-21, 142-43. *See also*
  Life cycles, insect

Leaf litter, 11-13, 24, 60, 92, 105,
  136, 169
Leaves, 3, 16-17, 57, 76, 124, 130,
  188; as food for insects and
  animals, 78-79, 119, 164
Leeches, 131-32.
Leeks, 59
Leverets, 165
Lichens, 86-87, 89, 176-79
Life cycles: animal, 91; insect, 11-12,
  78, 95, 97-100, 103, 105, 142-43,
  167; plant, 3, 123-25, 127-30, 173,
  174
Lightning bugs, 103
Little Dipper, 196
Lizards, 90
Lynx, 162, 164

Magnifying glass, 22, 177
Mammals, 3, 8-10, 13-14, 25-37, 119,
  140. *See also* Animals; names of
  individual mammals
Maple leaf cutters, 11
Maple sugaring, 27, 42-43, 60, 64,
  188
Maple trees, 30, 42-43, 164
Marmots, 27
Marten, 14, 162, 164
Mating: animal, 27-28, 33, 34-35, 53,
  60-62, 64, 155-56; insect, 94-95,
  103-106
Meadow mice, 9, 24, 53
Metamorphosis, 91, 97
Mice, 6, 8-9, 14, 30, 139, 146. *See
  also* Deer mice; Meadow mice
Midges, 122
Migration, bird, 44-46, 47, 65, 69
Millipedes, 87, 135-37
Mink, 9, 26, 162, 164
Mites, 87, 120
Mixed seeds, 5, 46
Moles, 9, 13, 24, 88, 133, 154, 156
Mollusks, 131-32
Molting, 44, 68, 69, 98, 163-64,
  184-85
Mosquitoes, 11, 93-96, 100
Mosses, 60, 87, 172-75, 176
Moths, 12, 78-80, 97, 122, 167-68
Mucus, 132-33, 153, 156
Mud, 10, 35, 112
Mushrooms, 59
Muskrats, 24

Nectar, 47, 109, 110, 125

208

Nematodes, 87, 120
Nests: insect, 11, 111-12, 114. *See also* Birds, nests of; Burrows; Dens
Newts, 90-92
Nocturnal animals, 157-59
North Star, 196
Nuthatches, 7, 12, 183, 192-94
Nutrients, 16, 86, 155
Nuts, 6, 69, 161, 170-71, 193
Nymphs, insect, 98-99

Oak trees, 122, 182
Orioles, 181
Otters, 26
Ovenbirds, 182
Owls, 6, 9, 33, 46, 140, 157, 164
Oxygen, 89, 104-105

Parasites, 121-22
Parsley family, 57, 124
Peepers, 60-62
Penguins, 185
Perennials, 15, 76, 117, 127
Pesticides, 94
Petals, 76, 107-109, 125
Pigeons, 7
Pileated woodpeckers, 12
Pine siskins, 5
Pistils, 77, 107-108
Pixie cups (plant), 176-77
Plants: as food for animals, 9-10, 56-59, 133-34, 136-37. *See also* Life cycles, plant; names of individual plants
Plumage, bird, 67, 70, 184-85
Poison hemlock, 57, 124
Poisonous plants, 57-59
Pollen, 47-48, 76, 108-109, 110, 125-26, 129-30, 189
Pollination, 47-48, 76, 108-109, 112, 125-26, 129, 189
Ponds, 35-36, 48, 60-64, 69-70, 98, 100
Porcupines, 9, 26-27, 30-33, 158, 190
Potatoes, 56
Prairie dogs, 25, 26-27
Praying mantises, 11
Predators, animals' protection against, 140, 143, 159, 162, 164, 167
Pupae, insect, 12, 95, 97, 113-14. *See also* Life cycles, insect
Purple finches, 44
Pussy willows, 47-49

Queen Anne's lace, 57, 123-26
Queens, insect, 11, 111-12, 114-15

Rabbits, 6, 9, 24, 30, 119, 159, 163-65
Raccoons, 8, 14, 30, 158
Raspberries, 117-19
Red efts, 90-92
Red-eyed vireos, 182-83
Redpolls, 5, 44-46
Reindeer "moss," 176
Reptiles, 3, 14, 91, 144
Rhubarb, 57
Robins, 65-66, 153, 180
Rocks, 86-89
Rodents, 26-29, 30, 121, 132, 144-49. *See also* Mice
Roots: of flowering plants, 74-75, 117, 120, 124, 130; of other plants, 87, 89, 173-74, 178; of trees, 3, 16, 23, 48, 188-89
Rose-breasted grosbeaks, 182
Roundworms, 88
Ruffed grouse, 6, 24, 53, 200

Salamanders, 90-92, 133
Scarlet tanagers, 181-82
Seedeaters (birds), 3-6, 83
Seeds, 23, 74, 76-77, 88, 108-109, 119, 126, 127; as food for birds and animals, 3-6, 8-9, 44-46, 69, 161, 193
Sepals, 77, 107-108
Setae, 153
Shrews, 9, 13, 133, 138-40, 154, 156
Shrikes, 46
Skunk cabbage, 57-58
Skunks, 8, 14, 30, 31, 154, 159, 167
Sleepers, winter, 8, 28. *See also* Hibernation; Hibernators
Slugs, 105, 131-34, 136, 154
Snails, 105, 131-33
Snakes, 91, 133, 144, 154, 162
Snow, 8, 14, 22-24, 35, 76, 164, 172
Snow fleas, 13-14
Social insects, 111-12, 113-16. *See also* Ants; Bees; Colonies, insect
Soil: as home for insects, 12, 13, 105, 136, 137; for plants, 16, 48, 86-89; formation of, 86-89, 133, 154-55, 176
Sparrows, 5, 7
Species, 26-27, 33, 77, 80, 83, 100, 109, 115. *See also* Survival (of species)

Spiders, 38-41, 69, 95, 110, 112, 144
Spores, 173
Spring: animals in the, 25, 28, 29, 33, 61-64, 153, 156; birds in the, 65-66, 68, 69, 71, 73, 180, 183, 185; insects in the, 11, 78, 79, 80, 105, 111, 112, 167; plants in the, 14, 23, 42-43, 47, 49, 74, 76, 127, 170, 188-89
Springtails, 14, 87
Squirrels, 9, 27, 30, 160-61, 170-71. *See also* Flying squirrels
Stalks, 57, 76, 108, 128
Stamens, 77, 107-108
Stars, 195-97
Stems, 120, 173-74
Succession (vegetation), 87
Suet, 5, 6, 18-19
Sugar bush, 53, 174, 179
Sugarhouse, 38-41
Summer: animals in the, 28, 63-64, 153, 163, 164; birds in the, 67-68, 69, 180, 187; insects in the, 79, 105, 113, 167; plants in the, 14, 117, 119, 126, 188
Sunflower seeds, 3, 5, 46, 184, 187, 193
Survival (of species), 33, 77, 85, 89, 116, 122, 126, 140, 143. *See also* Adaptations
Swallows, 21
Symbiosis, 178

Tadpoles, 98
Taproots, 74-75
Tent caterpillars, 78-80
Thistles, 186
Thrushes, 6, 182
Toads, 63, 133, 154
Tobacco, 57
Tomato plants, 56
Tracks, animal, 8-10, 29, 53-54
Tree frogs, 61
Trees, 3, 15-17, 19, 42-43, 49, 61-62, 87, 127; as food for animals,

30-31, 36; as homes for birds, 69; as homes for insects, 12, 78-80, 112; coniferous, 164, 181, 193; deciduous, 164, 181, 188-91. *See also* names of individual trees.
Tunnels, animal, 24, 53, 88, 160-61. *See also* Burrows; Dens
Turtles, 90, 133, 154
Twigs, 3, 15-17, 48, 188-89, 190; as food for insects and animals, 12, 24, 36, 164; as homes for insects, 12, 112, 120

Veeries, 182
Vixen, 53-54
Vultures, 145, 149

Walnuts, 170
Warblers, 6
Wasps, 13, 110-12, 113, 144
Weasels, 9, 26, 162, 164
Weeds, 77, 87, 109, 124-26
Weeping Willows, 49
Wild flowers, 107, 123-26
"Wild leeks," 59
Willows, 36, 47-49
Winter: animals in the, 8-10, 24, 27-28, 30, 33, 53-54, 156, 161, 164; birds in the, 3-7, 44-46, 184, 187; insects in the, 11-14, 78, 80, 111, 166, 168; plants in the, 15-17, 42-43, 47, 76, 127, 130, 188
Wood ducks, 37, 67-70, 184
Wood frogs, 60-62
Wood thrushes, 182
Woodchucks, 8, 25-29, 30, 161
Woodcocks, 71-73, 154
Woodpeckers, 5, 6, 12, 18-21, 37, 183, 192
Woolly bears, 166-68. *See also* Caterpillars
Workers, ant, 113-14
Wrens, 21

Yellow jackets, 111, 112

ABOUT THE AUTHOR

Gale Lawrence is a native of Springfield, Vermont. Born in 1941, she was educated at Earlham College where she received her B.A. degree and at Emory University where she received her M.A. degree. A free-lance writer, a teacher, and a naturalist, she writes a weekly nature column that appears in newspapers throughout Vermont.

Gale Lawrence lives in Huntington, Vermont.